yalsa
Young Adult Library
Services Association
www.ala.org/yalsa

Practical

Programming The Best of YA-YAAC

Monique Delatte Starkey

The paper used in this publication meets the minimum requirements of American National Standard for Information Sciences—Permanence of Paper for Printed Library Materials, ANSI Z39.48-1992. ∞

Library of Congress Cataloging-in-Publication Data applied for

Printed in the United States of America

17 16 15 14 13   5 4 3 2 1

ISBN: 978-0-8389-8670-7

Acknowledgments

Thank you to the devoted YALSA team, Beth Yoke, Jaclyn Finneke, Eve Gaus, Stephanie Kuenn, and Letitia Smith, who supported the development of this title, and who create professional development and educational opportunities for active, interested YALSA members; YALSA editors for preserving the voice of the book; YA-YAAC email list contributors who share programming ideas, planning advice, personal successes, and learning experiences to benefit both colleagues and young adult library users alike; and the teens that enthusiastically inspire librarians to push for innovative programs.

Personal appreciation to fountainheads Joseph and Gale Delatte for providing encouragement, advice, and free, top-notch editing; sposo David Starkey, who shared love, patience, and humor amid two summers of book writing; sibling Rachel Bezdek and cousin Renee Maccalupo Williams for time management tips; and long-time amies Vidhya Sriram Shelton, Lore Guilmartin, Pooja Jhunjhunwala, Thomas Johnson, Debbie Naughton, and Grisel Oquendo for marketing and outreach consultation.

Contents

Introduction

How? Why? When?

How Do I Conduct Programs for Teens?

If you've ever designed a young adult program from Adam's rib, then you are aware of the intrusiveness of unanticipated complications. Prepare thoroughly by considering the detailed programs that were selected for inclusion from the YA-YAAC email discussion list, an online tool sponsored by the Young Adult Library Services Association (YALSA). The list allows teen services professionals to share ideas about programming, teen advisory groups, professional development, and just about everything else.[1]

For librarians and library staffers who haven't kept up with the YA-YAAC discussion list religiously, **YALSA commissioned this book to investigate and outline the best new programming ideas found within YA-YAAC's archives through mid-2012**. This title complements previous YALSA titles by providing novel program inspiration as well as the nuts and bolts of how to successfully stage events. Even teen services advocates who have enjoyed the email discussion list since the late 1990s will appreciate the ease of perusal provided by this simply organized title. With more than 1,700 subscribers, the YA-YAAC email discussion list provides teen librarians with a cyber-water cooler—a 24/7 Web rendezvous for collaboration. The online resource is particularly useful for librarians serving

---

1. http://lists.ala.org/wws/arc/ya-yaac.

rural communities, those not working in goliath library systems, and others who may lack opportunities to connect with youth services colleagues to seek advice. YAACers freely contribute ideas, relate programming frustrations, and offer encouragement and success stories.

Librarians and other professionals who work with young adults consult the YA-YAAC list for a variety of reasons ranging from seeking practical advice for managing young adult services to searching for teen programming inspiration. Though this title focuses primarily on the list discourse regarding program ideas, also included are less easily cataloged items from deep within the YA-YAAC list annals. For example, teen services professionals often solicit tips for handling tricky situations and frequently request advice regarding managing the challenges inherent in providing young adult services. This book is designed to be inclusive of the wide assortment of issues that list contributors address. Programs included herein often begin with a question that a YAACer offered to the "great brain" (as the list is sometimes called by contributors). Sections may also start with definitions as several of the programs, such as LARPing (role-playing games in which participants embody characters) or parkour (physical training that integrates environmental obstacles), or employ terms with which readers may not be familiar. (Read on to learn more!) Though some terms used herein, like "lagniappe" (meaning "extra"), are not neologisms, these words include definitions to assist readers for whom the terms are unfamiliar.

"My manager wants me to start young adult outreach at my library, but there is no funding. What next?" This common YA-YAAC entreaty is regularly greeted by dozens of inspired, inexpensive programming ideas that are featured in Chapter 7 as "quickies." More in-depth program descriptions include the blueprint minutiae such as staff commitment, planning time, cost, and all of the necessary details. When available, modifications for differently-abled participants are noted. If planning time is at a minimum, consider the passive programming described in Chapter 1. Passive programming is a more self-directed approach that allows young adults to determine their level of participation. Chapter 2 offers active program ideas to get young adults moving. Book-themed programming is sprinkled throughout, but is also specifically addressed in Chapter 3. Nestled within Chapter 4 are the programs that best fit the category of educational and technological programming. Chapter 5 addresses the pop culture programs that teens scream for, including celebrity-themed celebrations. From Elvis Presley to Robert Pattinson, the tween and teen fervor for photogenic fellas is timeless, though the work of the individual artist of the moment may not endure. No matter who the current obsession is, simply alter the program ideas included in Chapter 5 to fit the hot celeb. After stuffing teens with the filler that is pop culture fandom, help YAs meet their daily allowance of fruits and vegetables with a heart-healthy salsa-making event. Food programs are so popular with young adults that Chapter 6 attempts to uncover fresh edible events that veteran YA librarians may not have previously hosted. With roughly three hundred posts each month, the list contributors take on a wide variety of concerns; therefore, Chapter 8 touches on advice for non-programming young adult services issues, including fundraising, program assessment, and event marketing.

Why Offer Teen Services?

Garnering support for teen services can feel like an uphill hike in pumps. Head inside, don your research fedora, and check the library charter, goals, and mission statement. You'll find that the library and the board of trustees have explicit mandates to serve the entire community—including young adults. Teens and their families pay taxes. Teens deserve equal service, and they *need* library services. After school, young people often lack supervision and the opportunity to participate in constructive activities.[2] The library can be a safe place for young people to spend time after school, so teens are often already in or around the library, hanging out, meeting friends, skating, killing time. Developing successful teen programming is a way to reach out to (and keep tabs on) the young adults who are already in and around the library. Remind the naysayers that outreach to young adults will increase the control that the library has over teens that are already present. Caution the teen haters, too, that young patrons grow up to be the local business owners, government officials, and voters who either support libraries, or who question the relevance of libraries in the information era.

Teen outreach strengthens ties to the community. Parents, patrons, local businesses, and politicos recognize that role, and appreciate libraries that work to provide outreach to young adults. Yet it can be difficult to convince coworkers and library friends to support teen programming. The library charter doesn't state that outreach to the community excludes the young adult crowd, but it can seem as though some folks interpret it that way. Looking for an enjoyable way to address this challenge? Help the doubters share their culture with teens. For example, try a simple food program in which young people learn how to prepare a no-bake traditional dish. Cultural programming that incorporates the interests and backgrounds of library staffers affirms for the library team that their contribu-

---

2. Daud, Ranna, and Cynthia Carruthers. 2008. "Outcome Study of an After-School Program for Youth in a High-Risk Environment." *Journal of Park & Recreation Administration* 26, no. 2: 95-114. *Academic Search Complete*, EBSCO*host* (accessed December 29, 2012).

tions are appreciated, that working with teens is fun, and that the next generation is essential to passing along cultural folkways.

Is the library director or manager open to allowing the more responsible teens to help with less complex library tasks? If so, there is another great way to grow appreciation of young people: Train teens to assist with jobs like shelf-reading and summer reading program implementation. More teen volunteerism ideas can be found throughout this book, particularly Chapters 1 and 7. Appendix 1 contains teen volunteer application form templates.

When Do I Start?

Starting up young adult programming isn't always easy. The YA-YAAC discussion list is a reliable repository for exceptional programming ideas. This book addresses the teen librarian need as expressed via tweet by YA and Readers' Advisory Paralibrarian Rachelle: "Trying to search YA-YAAC archives. Nearly ready to peel my eyelids off in frustration. Why is this so hard?"[3] Rather than braving the *palpebra*-peeling frustration of searching a clunky archive, flip through the best programs by browsing this compendium *right now!*

---

3. http://twitter.com/#!/ruhshellmc/status/27773697343356928.

Passive Programs

Passive, or self-directed, programs are all the rage among YAAC-ers balancing funding cuts with the commitment to outreach to young adults. As budget shortfalls and staffing cutbacks lead to reduced services, passive programming represents the most viable option for many. These low-maintenance, self-guided programs reduce the need for adult supervision.

Looking for some new programming ideas... I am going to promote the photo contest, but our library doesn't have cameras or photo editing technology that the teens could actually use, so it's not very interactive... Any ideas that fit the theme?—Youth Services Librarian Kara Honaker Bourn, Livingston Parish Library System, Albany-Springfield Branch

PROGRAM

Virtual Scavenger Hunt

Description

"Teens are provided with a list of ten well-known, fictional locations,"[1] offers Youth Services Associate Tinna Mills, Chippewa River District Library, Mount Pleasant, Michigan. "Their job is to figure out which book

---

1. Mills posted the following locations: Forks, Hogwarts, Camp Half Blood, Camp Green Lake, Green Gables, the Capitol, New Pretty Town, Alagaesia, Fell's Church, and the Shire.

(or book series) each location is from, then find or take a picture of the book covers, and upload them to a photo-sharing site such as Photobucket or Flickr. They then send a link to their photo album to the librarian via e-mail, and are entered into a drawing for prizes." Mills describes the contest as a month-long program slated for the slower programming month of August.

At Jefferson County Public Library, Jenna Obee "provided a list of items that teens needed to photograph, like 'something dark' and 'your favorite library.'[2] They combined the photos into a mosaic, and submitted the picture to the library." Obee explains, "During Teen Tech Week, we posted the entries and allowed votes for the best. The winning entries were displayed on our blog and in our libraries."

Steps

Before

"We brainstormed the idea at a meeting of the Teen Advocates Round Table, the committee that oversees services for teens in our library system," details Obee. "Our technology representative wrote the memo, and had our management liaison refine it. It was approved by management. Then we wrote content for the blog and library website, which the Web department posted. This included a form for entries."

During

Obee shares, "Some of our Teen Advisory Boards created their mosaics during meetings, which used the library's cameras and computers. Otherwise it was all done outside of the library."

After

"After the entries were collected, the library's Web department created a website with the entries and a poll," says Obee. "We then wrote a blog announcing the winners and our graphics department created a poster highlighting the top three entries. The posters were displayed in the teen areas at each of the libraries."

---

2. Obee's teens searched for: "new technology, old technology, something so last year, something beautiful, something sad, something green, something fuzzy, something dark, a visual representation of your favorite book, your favorite library, and what's in your future."

Cost

Inexpensive

- Staff time:
    - "It's an idea that we can run at all five of our branches without devoting extra staff time to running events during a month with typically lower attendance," notes Mills.
    - "[Our costs were] only staff," Obee says. "We anticipated spending about 5-10 hours to plan and implement the program, including time for our Web folks to get it posted. The graphics department spent time designing a poster of the winners and printing it for each library."
- Program costs:
    - Explains Obee, "We wanted to do something online for Teen Tech Week, but had no budget for a program. Instead we simply posted instructions on the Web, and encouraged participation."

Program Type

- Passive
- Great for tweens *and* teens

Duration

One month

Planning Time

2-8 hours

Marketing

Rather than the library simply promoting the program for Jefferson County Public Library, the *program* actually promoted the library. Says Obee, "We had twelve entries from a variety of teens from our county (http://engagedpatrons.org/Blogs.cfm?SiteID=2367&BlogID=224&BlogPostID=6326). We received 363 votes. Having information about the program on our new blog increased visibility of the blog." Obee describes how the *library* also marketed the program: "The winners were proud to have their art displayed in the library."

Feedback

"We had a discussion about what went well, and what could be improved," says Obee. "We decided to do a video contest, asking teens to create a video about summer reading."

Raves

"According to the MacArthur Foundation," muses Obee, "research shows that young people participate in social and recreational online activities that can be a springboard for learning. In this program, we sought to help our teen patrons strengthen the technical and social skills they'll need to succeed in the 21st century by enabling them to engage directly with digital technologies." She adds, "This program was designed to capture their imagination, expand their digital skills, enable them to create and share their own content, and interact with their peers on a topic of mutual interest."

Mills affirms, "I would definitely be willing to try something like this again as the cost to the library was minimal."

Web Component

"They must either take photos of physical books that they find in the collection, or use a computer to locate an image of the cover online," says Mills.

Tips

Obee recommends the link http://gcplteens.blogspot.com/2009/07/digital-photo-scavenger-hunt.html. Mill mentions that one teen created a Word document containing all of the photos and attached that to an e-mail, which was just as successful as the online folder submissions.

Lagniappe[3] (Extra)

How did YA-YAAC influence Mills' program? "I got the idea when someone on YA-YAAC was brainstorming popular places in YA lit for a display he/she was doing at their library," says Mills. "YA-YAAC also helped me come up with ideas to streamline the process for submission of photos."

Photos

View all three winners of Jefferson County Public Library's photo scavenger hunt via: http://engagedpatrons.org/Blogs.cfm?SiteID=2367&BlogID=224&BlogPostID=6577&Comment=Y

---

3.   "Lagniappe, n.**Pronunciation:** /læˈnjæp/ **Etymology:** Louisiana French, < Spanish *la ñapa*, in the same sense.*U.S.* Something given over and above what is purchased, earned, etc., to make good measure or by way of gratuity." "lagniappe, n.". OED Online. June 2012. Oxford University Press. http://www.oed.com/view/Entry/105095?redirectedFrom=lagniappe (accessed August 09, 2012).

Virtual scavenger hunt winning entry by Artist Dominique Silverman, age 16.

Origami

origami
Pronunciation: Brit. /ˌɒrɪˈgɑːmi/ , *U.S.* /ˌɔrəˈgɑmi/
Etymology: < Japanese origami

The Japanese art of folding paper into intricate decorative designs and objects; paper folded in this way.

1961 E. Kallop in S. Randlett Art of Origami (1963) 16 Apart from origami as an art in the sense of the individually unique, folded paper has a role in the ceremonial etiquette of Japanese life.[4]

Description

"A reduced budget at my library prevents me from actually holding programs for teens, so I'm offering a passive program consisting of a series of make-and-take crafts," posts Teen Services Librarian Allison Tran. For the Mission Viejo Library's month-long summer reading program, Tran offers a different travel-themed craft each week. The "boredom busters" projects include a matchbox Louvre, origami, island trip magnets, and miniature scrapbooks.

---

4.   origami, n. Oxford Dictionaries, third edition, September 2004; OED Online, September 2011. Oxford University Press. http://www.oed.com/view/Entry/132555 (accessed September 17, 2011). An entry for this word was first included in A Supplement to the OED III, 1982.

Supplies

Solid and patterned origami paper, origami books, and instructional/informational handouts.

Steps
Before

- Clear a space at the reference desk and wrap that area in colorful art paper. Tran designates this area as the "Boredom Busters Zone."
  - "Hosting these crafts at the reference desk is great because it's an opportunity to interact with the teens, and make them feel welcome in their library. It's also convenient for keeping an eye out for spontaneous glitter fights. Not that my library teens would ever do that! I'm just saying."
- Tran consulted PBS[5] and Kids Web Japan.[6]

During

Supply reference desk colleagues with information about the passive program. Demonstrate the teen/tween craft for coworkers if possible. "Since I'm not always at the reference desk, I e-mail my colleagues each week to explain the craft, note the location of extra supplies, and so on," Tran says, "It's all about communication!"

Cost

$15-$100

Program Type

Passive

Duration

Four weeks

Planning Time

2-6 hours

Marketing

Art supplies displayed in an open workspace passively tempt participants. Tran also posts programs to her blog.[7]

---

5. http://www.pbs.org/independentlens/between-the-folds/history.html
6. http://web-japan.org/kidsweb/virtual/origami/origami01.html
7. http://readingeverywhere.blogspot.com/

YA Involvement

Schedule teen volunteers at the reference desk crafting space to assist peers or tweens with projects.

Partnerships

Connect with local scrapbooking, art supply, or stationery stores to coordinate origami paper donation. Check with management to see if a sign can be posted near the crafting area to acknowledge the contribution.

Raves

"I debuted the Boredom Busters last year, and they were a hit," Tran promises.

Web Component

Check out samples posted by Tran: http://readingeverywhere.blogspot.com/search/label/summer%20reading

Lagniappe

"It bears mentioning that when working with Mod Podge...dole it out in small containers," Tran cautions. "Just, um, trust me on this."

Additional Passive Programs

- Cover young adult area tables in colorful kraft or butcher paper. Place crayons in bowls on the tables. Cost: $10-$30.
- Encourage tweens and teens to submit book or movie reviews to the library blog or social networking site. Comments Frances Veit of Buckham Memorial Library, "I have [teens] write and e-mail me book reviews of the books they're reading. This works out great—they get good feelings for volunteering, and I get teen reviews to put on our teen blog and Goodreads page. It's very hands-off and they can even do it from home."
  - Posting to the list from Australia, Mosman Library Promotions and Youth Services Librarian Alycia Bailey suggests, "You could get them to choose a book out of the group of books that have been challenged, and write a short bit on why they think it's important to keep [it] available in libraries. Post up the responses to websites or social networking sites." Bailey then urges, "Make a display using book cover images and their handwriting...Voila!"

Wrap tables in young adult space with disposable paper, and make available a crayon basket. Instant fun. Photograph by Monique Delatte Starkey

- "When I have teens approach me during the school year," Veit says, "if they're crafty, I have them help with board stories for story time, or set up a craft for kids."
  - Apply online for the Target early childhood reading grant, which opens annually in April. This $2,000 grant can provide read-aloud materials for events such as teen-led read-a-thons. (Find more information at https://corporate.target.com/corporate-responsibility/grants/early-childhood-reading-grants)
- Responding to an entreaty for ideas posted to the email discussion list by a self-described newbie, Trumbull Library's Sandra Miller suggests passive programming, specifically, "putting games and puzzles out in their area."
  - Approach local bookstores, toy stores, and comic book stores to request the donation of new board games or puzzles. Library friends, community members, and staff members may also be interested in giving new or used games and puzzles. Via the circulation or reference desk, check out the games for in-library use. Award teen mentors volunteer hours for playing board games with library kids.

Young adult volunteers prepare crafts for La Puente Library story time participants. Photograph by Monique Delatte Starkey

Tweens compete in the classic card game UNO, a donation from Barnes and Noble. Photograph by Monique Delatte Starkey

Sidebars

Board and Card Game Ideas for Teens

- Apples to Apples
- Scattergories
- Fluxx (Amigo Spiele) & Zombie Fluxx
- Run for Your Life
- Candyman
- Munchkin
- UNO
- Monopoly
- High School Musical
- Clue
- Jenga
- Ingenious (Fantasy Flight Games)
- Pictureka
- Battleship (not electronic)
- Hangman
- Killer Bunnies
- Settlers of Catan
- Once Upon a Time
- Pictionary
- Bingo
- Pretty Pretty Princess
- Connect 4
- Boggle
- Guess Who
- No Stress Chess
- Mancala
- Taboo
- Topple
- Man Bites Dog
- Pit
- ASAP
- Bananagrams
- Outburst
- Blockus
- Ticket to Ride
- Quelf

Photograph by Monique Delatte Starkey

Puff Pong

Directions:

1. Gather around a table. Round tables work best.
2. Make your goal with a pointer finger from each hand. Your R finger touches the L finger of your neighbor. Your L finger touches the R finger of your other neighbor. All edges of the table are someone's goal.
3. Eat a breath mint. Bad breath is a foul.
4. Put the pong ball in the middle of the table.
5. Place your mouth near the edge of the table and puff. Your face may never hover over the table. Stay off the edge, not over it. Make other players laugh to weaken their defense. No spitting.
6. If the ball rolls off your goal, STRIKE ONE.
7. Three strikes and you are out.
8. After striking out, everyone else makes their goal larger.
9. Continue until only one remains.

Courtesy of Kimberly Bolan & Associates, LLC Indianapolis, IN

Board Game Event Tips (Tongue-in-Cheek)

ADVERTISING

- THIS IS WHERE YOU MAKE YOUR MONEY. GO TO THE SCHOOLS! TELL YOUR TAB TO TELL 5 FRIENDS. AND TELL THOSE 5 FRIENDS TO TELL 5 FRIENDS. BUT STOP THERE BECAUSE THAT'S ALREADY WAY TOO MANY KIDS TO DEAL WITH.

THE NERDIEST OF THE NERD GAMES!!!

- THESE ARE THE COOLEST GAMES OF THEM ALL! EXAMPLES INCLUDE BUT ARE NOT LIMITED TO:
  - CARCASSONE
  - RA
  - COSMIC ENCOUNTER
  - SETTLERS OF CATAN
  - AXIS & ALLIES
  - EVERY GAME EVER MADE IN GERMANY (SERIOUSLY)

Board Game Event Tips (Tongue-in-Cheek)

SAMPLE SETUP FOR Y'ALL

GAME #1

GAME #2 AND/OR #3 IF BIG ENOUGH

SNACK TABLE!!! THEY LOVE THIS TABLE

Courtesy of Los Angeles librarians Josh Irwin and Jose Parra

2

No Sweat!
Active Programs

As school districts slash funding for physical education classes,[1] libraries are tapping into teen interest in active programming. In this chapter, readers will find kinetically-engaging activities like Nerf turf wars, parkour training, and more.

Kids are asking for a parkour program—freerunning stunts. They want a demonstration and would like to learn some moves. Has anyone done this?—Head Librarian Kristen M. Corby, Periodicals and Young Adult Division, New Orleans Public Library

PROGRAM

Parkour: The Art of Movement

parkour, n.

Pronunciation: Brit. /pɑːˈkɔː/ , U.S. /ˌpɑrˈkɔ(ə)r/

Etymology: < French parkour, altered spelling of parcours parcours n. *The discipline or activity of moving rapidly and freely over or around the obstacles presented by an (esp. urban) environment by running, jumping, climbing, etc.*

---

1. Toporek, Bryan. "Survey Finds Drop In P.E. Classes, But Increase in Sports." *Education Week* 31, no. 26 (March 28, 2012): 11. Academic Search Premier, EBSCOhost (accessed August 6, 2012).

2005 Globe & Mail (Toronto) 28 May m3/1 (heading) In the growing discipline of parkour, railings become gymnastics bars and trash cans become vault boxes as adrenaline junkies treat the city as their playground. [2]

Description

"Don't walk around obstacles; use them to move through your surroundings," explains Kris Chipps of Arapahoe Library District. "The presenter [we used]…is a highly-trained traceur, owner of his own business, and in multiple videos demonstrating parkour." When YAACers expressed concern about the safety of parkour, Chipps clarified, "He showed videos, explained the difference between parkour and free running, and stressed safety and basic moves. He brought sawhorses of varying heights, and demonstrated in slow motion how to use them to get from one point to another. All teens had the opportunity to use the moves he taught. They loved it!"

Young Adult Librarian Bonnie Svitavsky says, "We have a park right in front of the building, with wide open grassy spaces, along with a bandstand and a series of cement blocks designed to look like books. This was a great space for them to use. They started out teaching the teens about stretching and warming up. They did a variety of jumping drills, on and off grass. The drills weren't very elaborate. I think anyone who's relatively fit could do them." Her group then transported the blocks to the library entrance area. "They showed the teens how to jump from one to the other and to land quietly (this is more about safety and doing it right, not being loud)." Svitavsky's program next relocated to the bandstand where "teens were shown other moves, such as using the railing, corners, ledges, and steps."

Svitavsky observes, "Throughout the program, the instructors kept reminding them about being safe while working and only doing moves that the teens were comfortable with, moving at your own pace, and being aware of your surroundings." She notes that the traceurs recommended practice: "This was not a romanticized version of parkour, but lots of drills that included crawling, jumping, and lifting yourself up and over low walls and railings."

"They ended with talking about how to improve your balance," Svitavsky recollects. "An instructor gave an example of standing on one foot while brushing your teeth and closing your eyes to make it more difficult."

---

2   "parkour, n.". OED Online. June 2012. Oxford University Press. http://www.oed.com/view/Entry/276444?redirectedFrom=parkour (accessed August 09, 2012).

Lastly, "They invited the teens to try walking along a rail, which goes up a sloping ramp. Instructors and I would stand on either side of the teens and offer hands to balance them." Following the parkour, "They did more stretching to cool down, talked about being respectful of property, and answered questions."

Program Type

Active, high-energy
- The emphasis is on parkour basics," stresses Svitavsky. "No climbing sides of building or leaping over cars. This is more about teaching them an alternate way to exercise and, in keeping with the summer theme, exploring the world around you."

Cost

- Varies. $100-$250, depending on cost of parkour trainers and staff involvement (as many as four staffers may be needed).

Duration

1-3 hours

Planning Time

Varies depending on marketing, partnering research, but averages 6-10 hours.

Marketing

- Svitavsky marketed the program by building it with library teens. She writes, "My teens asked for a program that involved dancing or a cool type of exercise. Originally the request was something along the lines of Zumba. It gradually morphed into finding someone to teach parkour."

Steps
Before

- Find a parkour program provider. "We work about eight months ahead of when a program is presented," says Chipps. "This allows time for our communications department to produce the publicity pieces for our patrons."
- Market the event.

- "Prep the teens," Svitavsky urges. "The exercises were strenuous over time, and most teens didn't wear the right clothes or shoes." She also suggests reminding teens to bring water.
- Determine a funding source. Svitavsky put the cost at "about $200 ($10 per teen). This fee was paid through our Friends of the Library group."
- Create and distribute permission forms. "I set out a signup list/permission forms at the same desk where teens and kids sign up for our summer reading program," says Svitavsky.

Immediately Prior

- Work with traceur to set up equipment. Check that all participants have turned in permission forms.
- Svitavsky says, "On the day of the event, I set up a meeting room as a starting point. We talked about some of the parkour books in the library's collection and then we moved outside to begin the program."

After

Pass out comment forms to teens.

YA Involvement

"All the teens could participate as frequently as they liked." Chipps notes that the presenter "stayed up to a half an hour after the program to talk to any teen who had questions."

Partnerships

- "If you check with a local college or gym for the name of someone who does this, you may find they'll do it for very little cost," although Chipps cautions, "Be careful with that. Really check their philosophy and what they'd teach a beginner."
  - Svitavsky contacted a local group that teaches parkour in Seattle/Tacoma. "We have a large park in front of our library, so there's a lot of room to run," she says of her location, Puyallup Public Library. "We're partnering with our city's parks department." The "parks and rec department…was able to help supervise and keep the area clear." Svitavsky's permission form was provided by the traceurs.

Safety First

Dione Basseri of Northern California urges, "Besides permission slips, I'd recommend having the instructor give a very frank talk about dangers and injuries, and institute a zero-tolerance policy."

Tween and Teen Librarian Chrissie Morrison demurred, saying, "You could not pay me enough to take on the responsibility of having a program like that."

"While it sounds like fun, it also sounds like a liability nightmare!" concurs Collection Development/Teen Services Librarian Courtney Waters.

Chipps addresses the safety concerns of YAACers:

I have to chime in with a huge *do it*!

I did a parkour program for 3 of our libraries several years ago, and the teens loved it. Our instructor has his own company in Denver, has taken advanced training by the people in France who began this movement, and absolutely insisted on safety. The teens didn't do anything without his okay. He worked on basics: what parkour and freerunning are and what they are not. He had them stretching and working on becoming more limber. He brought in sawhorses of different heights, and began with the shortest one, gradually going higher. He showed them how to cross over an obstacle, and there is definitely a right and wrong way to do this! If any teen didn't feel like attempting something, he didn't insist.

While some teens may have been disappointed in not learning how to do back-flips off cars (though they never let on!), all who attended were courteous, respectful, worked hard, and took every tip he gave them to heart.

We didn't require permission slips, and all was good. There were at least 3 adults in the room, the instructor and 2 staff members. Limit the number who can attend, though, just to give each one of them plenty of time to practice moves. We capped at 15.

Svitavsky considered YAACers concerns, then replied, "Am I nervous about it? Yeah. Am I nervous about almost all my programs before they happen? Yeah! And having to deal with things like food allergies at my anime program last week, teens crashing into each other at a water balloon fight last year, and using sharp objects for duct tape/T-shirt altering/paper crafts. I feel like this is just another program. I hope."

Feedback

Chipps says, "We have an evaluation form to be filled out by staff, and a form that teens complete. The staff form asks for input on the presenter." Chipps' staff evaluation forms rate "skills, knowledge, how well material was presented," while teens forms include "what they thought of the program, what they liked best about it, what they liked least." These comments are also passed on to the presenter.

Raves

- "I loved having this program. It's different, current, active, and appeals to both genders. Plus, the sheer awesomeness of what trained traceurs can do is amazing. I could watch for hours!" declares Chipps.
- "I would absolutely do this program again," Svitavsky affirms. "We saw many new faces. We got a local business involved with the library. We taught teens about physical fitness and respect for community and property. I can't think of many programs that get a lot of teen guys into the library that also cover those subjects!"

Resources

Chipps consulted:

- www.apexmovement.com
- www.americanparkour.com
- www.coloradoparkour.com
- YouTube parkour videos

Lagniappe

"Have a table with books and other media that teens can check out," advises Chipps.

Photos

Visit these sites to view photos and videos posted by YAACers from library parkour events:

> http://www.flickr.com/photos/puyalluplibrary/sets/72157627256698496/
> http://www.facebook.com/media/set/?set=a.10150261724612355.331194.325099737354
> http://www.youtube.com/watch?v=kG1vXOgMhQk

Circle Game Quickie

I am doing my first after-hours lock-in for teens," posts Youth Services Librarian Celine Swan of Grand Public Library. "I am thinking pizza and pop and maybe a movie. Does anyone play any fun games?

Description

Originally posted by the YALSA Fiscal Office's Penny Johnson, this competition is adaptable to nearly any party occasion. Cindy Simerlink of Dayton Metro Library weighs in, "I've used Penny's game at least ten times

now, and teens always love it! It's a great way to help fill out a themed party."

Teen, Tween, and Young Adult Specialist Penny Johnson explains, "In advance, 40-50 trivia questions are gathered. The answers to all of the questions are printed on wordstrips, one answer per strip. Create a complete set of wordstrips for each team." The Baraboo Public Library specialist writes, "Participants are divided into 3-4 teams. Each team receives a set of wordstrips, which they spread out on a table or on the floor for all team members to see. Place 3-4 chairs in the front of the room, equal distance from the teams. Label each chair with a point value (e.g. 100/200/500). The moderator asks the first question. All of the teams search their wordstrips for the proper answer. When they find the correct strip, they send a runner to sit in a chair." She adds, "If the runner has the proper answer, his/her team receives the points for that chair. If the answer is wrong, the points are deducted." How does the game end? Johnson laughs, "When all questions have been asked, add up the scores and crown the winner!"

"Thanks for posting that game," YA Librarian Kathleen Gruver replied to Johnson, "It has been a big hit." She shares, "We're even doing a zombie trivia version at our upcoming lock-in, to go along with our Humans vs. Zombies theme." (Gruver's zombie trivia questions are appended to this section.)

"A big thank you from the teens in Leominster; they just LOVE this game," types Young Adult Services Coordinator Diane Sanabria. She offers a cushy alternative: "We now have them race to huge lounge pillows from our loft." Simerlink's YAs have a ball when playing the circle game, as she confesses, "I use it all the time and the teens always enjoy it so much. I'm not sure how many times I've played it…I've done horror movies, Twilight, ice cream, pizza, chocolate, Halloween costumes, Harry Potter, a black hole/space one, villains, and maybe one or two others." The librarian reveals, "There's a real art to developing and arranging the questions."

Simerlink provides her ice cream trivia game as an example:

About how many licks does it take to eat a scoop of ice cream?	50
Colored, flavored, and frozen water is called what?	Popsicle
How many UDF (United Dairy Farmer) stores are there in Ohio?	175
How much of the volume of ice cream is air?	50%
Ice cream was first sold around local neighborhoods in trucks owned by what company?	Good Humor
In 2006, what one country ate more ice cream per person than the United States?	New Zealand
Most popular flavor	Vanilla
Name the flavor: chocolate ice cream with marshmallow, caramel, and fudge fish.	Phish Food
Name the flavor: made with Oreos.	Cookies 'n' cream
The earliest written record of an ice cream-like dessert comes from what country?	China
The Guinness world record for largest ice cream cake was set in 2005 by what company?	Carvel
Name the flavor: chocolate ice cream, cherry ice cream, cherries, chocolate flakes, and brownie chunks.	Jerry's Jubilee

The slogan "Ice Cream of the Future" is used by what ice cream company?	Dippin' Dots
The world's most expensive sundae costs $1,000 and is served in a restaurant in New York. It features caviar and what other special ingredient?	Gold
This ingredient is required in order for it to be a turtle sundae.	Caramel sauce
What company specializes in flavors for the grown-up palate?	Haagen-Dazs
What do you call the treat that's a block of ice cream between two graham crackers or cookies?	Ice cream sandwich
What do you put on top of a "pretty please?"	A cherry
What percent of U.S. households buy ice cream?	98%
What is America's favorite ice cream topping?	Chocolate syrup
What percentage of the stuff must be milkfat in order to fit the legal definition of "ice cream??"	10%
What state has the most Dairy Queens?	Texas
What's the rest of this advertising slogan: What would you do for a _____?	Klondike Bar
What state produces the third most ice cream in the U.S.?	Ohio
What treat is made by dipping an ice cream bar in chocolate?	Eskimo Pie
What U.S. city buys the most ice cream per person?	Portland
What year did the first American ice cream parlor open?	1776
Name the flavor: chocolate ice cream, vanilla ice cream, fudge brownies, choc chip cookie dough.	Half Baked
When did the first commercial ice cream plant open?	1851
Where is most vanilla grown?	Madagascar

Answer slips shared by Simerlink:

Caramel sauce	Caramel sauce	Caramel sauce
A cherry	A cherry	A cherry
Chocolate syrup	Chocolate syrup	Chocolate syrup
Gold	Gold	Gold
China	China	China
Madagascar	Madagascar	Madagascar
New Zealand	New Zealand	New Zealand
Ohio	Ohio	Ohio
Texas	Texas	Texas
Portland	Portland	Portland
10%	10%	10%
50%	50%	50%
98%	98%	98%
50	50	50
175	175	175
1776	1776	1776
1851	1851	1851
Cookies 'n' cream	Cookies 'n' cream	Cookies 'n' cream
Half Baked	Half Baked	Half Baked

Jerry's Jubilee	Jerry's Jubilee	Jerry's Jubilee
Phish Food	Phish Food	Phish Food
Vanilla	Vanilla	Vanilla
Eskimo Pie	Eskimo Pie	Eskimo Pie
Ice cream sandwich	Ice cream sandwich	Ice cream sandwich
Klondike Bar	Klondike Bar	Klondike Bar
Popsicle	Popsicle	Popsicle
Carvel	Carvel	Carvel
Dippin' Dots	Dippin' Dots	Dippin' Dots
Good Humor	Good Humor	Good Humor
Haagen-Dazs	Haagen-Dazs	Haagen-Dazs

Instructions for Numbered Chairs Trivia Game

Divide the group up into teams (ideally 3 teams although, 2-5 will work, with 3-10 people per team) and give each team a table to spread out the answer slips. At the head of the room, put one chair for each team. Mark each chair with a point value—suggested points are 10,000, 5,000, and 1,000. Moderator reads a question. The team chooses the answer that they believe matches the question, and hands it to their runner, who dashes for the chairs. If they're sure of the answer, they head for the high point value chair; if they're unsure, they go for the lowest. After the dust has settled and all the chairs have a person in them, the answer slips are compared to the right answer. If a team is right, they get the points for the chair they're sitting in; if they're wrong, the points are subtracted.

Optional rule: Every 5 questions, the runner must change.

Optional rule: Every 5 questions, the team in last place may choose a player to "steal" from another team.

To use this file: Cut apart the answers on sheet 2 (print twice if needed), and give one set to each team. Print sheet 1 for the moderator.

This game is so much fun because even people who don't know the trivia can help by running, keeping the slips organized, searching for the right one once someone has hissed "blue!", etc., and of course the running gets the adrenaline high. I find it's helpful to have someone besides me do the scorekeeping. It's also fun to have the teams give themselves names and then use those crazy names as often as possible.

Courtesy of Cindy Simerlink, Teen Librarian, Huber Heights Branch, Dayton Metro Library, Ohio

Senior Librarian for Teen Services Patricia Foster posts a circle game adaptation: "All the teens get in a big circle, each on a chair, with one teen left over to stand in the middle. The teen in the middle says something they have NOT done, or someplace they have NOT been, etc. Anyone who has done it or been there has to change chairs. They can't just move to the one next to theirs—it has to be a different chair at least partway across the circle. It's a great fill-in game, good for any occasion where you may have teens waiting for an activity, or you have finished all your activities too soon and have time left at your lock-in." Foster offers one last plug: "It's a good get-acquainted game, too. You will find a lot of the same teens getting stuck in the middle, and others who never get there."

Foster's examples include, "I have never been to Disneyland, I have never played soccer, I have never had red hair, I am not wearing a red shirt, I have never broken my leg. Anyone who has been to Disneyland, played soccer, has had red hair, or is wearing a red shirt, or who has broken their leg has to change chairs."

According to Foster, Herriman Public Library teens don't think that the circle game is just for squares. "We have played it for almost two hours, and then I have had to insist that we do something else." Perhaps the greatest endorsement: "Even teens who are reluctant at first to join the game will eventually grab a chair...They love it."

PROGRAM

Nerf Turf Wars (a.k.a. Humans vs. Zombies)

My brother competed in Nerf turf wars on his college campus. Could the library host humans vs. zombies?

Nerf

Pronunciation: Brit. /nəːf/ , U.S. /nərf/
Etymology: *Apparently an arbitrary formation, although perhaps compare nerf v.*

A type of foam rubber used esp. in the manufacture of children's toys and sports equipment.

1986 J. Updike Roger's Version (1987) 79 These young people come at you with their drawn sword of youth and it turns out to be a rubber prop, a nerf sword.[3]

Description

The library is transformed from a proud bastion of learning into a fierce theater of war. In tromp the teenaged, painted for battle, aggressively wielding Nerf battle gear. At Curtis Memorial Library in Brunswick, Maine, young adults in the sixth through twelfth grades compete in games staged throughout the library, including capture the flag (humans vs. zombies). The lucky YAs served by Teen Librarian Melissa Orth appreciate this program so immensely that the library has staged six competitions in the last eighteen months.

Alternatively, libraries can try a Zombie Survival Seminar, as staged by Tammy Blackwell at Marshall County Public Library, in Calvert City, Kentucky. Blackwell writes, "The Zombie Survival Seminar was based on the book *The Zombie Survival Guide* by Max Brooks. The first part of the program involved 'trained professionals' presenting the truth behind the zombie virus, how to recognize the living dead, and how to fend off the zombies. The second half of the program was dedicated to hands-on training with Nerf guns and an opportunity to take on online zombie survival quiz."

Quick and Dirty: How to Play

(As staged by Samantha Marker, Mount Laurel Library, New Jersey).

Object of Game

In a library usurped by zombies, the humans must complete a mission.

Mission

Find and retrieve a hidden object (or objects).

Game 1: Steps/Rules of Play

1. Create a mission card containing the mission, one hint about object placement, and one hint as to the identity of the object. Provide the card to humans.
2. Divide teens into teams; all players will be allowed an opportunity to act as humans by the end of the program.

Alternative: All but four participants are released from safe zone to begin acting as zombies, then four humans are released to retrieve objects.

3. Using bandannas or flags (as in flag football), if a zombie snags a human's flag, that human is bitten. Once bitten, the human surrenders weapons, and becomes a zombie.
4. Using Nerf darts (or by tossing rolled-up socks), humans shoot zombies. Once hit, the stunned zombies must remain still for fifteen seconds.

Winning

Retrieving the object = mission accomplished.
All humans turned into zombies = epic fail.

Game 2: Steps/Rules of Play

(As staged by Melissa Orth, Curtis Memorial Library, Brunswick, Maine.)

1. Prior to participant arrival:
   • Volunteer teens prepare name tags. Half of the names tags will be blue ink, half red ink.
   • Place several objects, such as soda cans and plastic water bottles, in out-of-reach library areas.
2. Select team names and captains.
3. Teams have ten minutes to locate and shoot down objects, then return to safe area with objects.

Simple Alternative: Steps/Rules of Play

1. Assign one participant to the role of zombie.
2. This participant leaves the safe area first with a two-minute lead.
3. Zombie pulls a human's bandana to transform that human into a zombie.
4. Participants shoot Nerf bullets to stun zombies (who drop to the ground for three seconds). *Note: Players may not always feel the bullets, which can cause confusion.*

Even Simpler Alternative: Steps/Rules of Play

Free-for-all Nerf gun battle. Play first as teams, then as individuals.

Cost

• Staff time
• Optional supplies (Blackwell spent $50 on her program):

- Flags (or participant-supplied bandannas)
- Zombie makeup
- Library- or participant-supplied rolled socks or Nerf gear (guns, darts, apparel)

Program Type

Active

- Says Marker, "Physical programs where teens are allowed to run in the library have a successful track record at my library."
- "It is fun! It gets guys into the library," says Orth. "It is active, since we do allow running. It requires teamwork and problem-solving."

Duration

Ranges from 1 hour to all night long

Planning Time

Varies, 1-10 hours

Marketing

Wiki, word-of-mouth

Steps (Extended Version)

As suggested by Melissa Orth, Curtis Memorial Library, Brunswick, Maine, and Samantha Marker, Mount Laurel Library, New Jersey.

Before

- Work with teens to:
  - Plan program.
  - Develop rules.
  - Determine marketing plan with teen advisory board (TAB).
- Coordinate with staff and management to:
  - Secure management support for an after-hours program.
  - Select referee(s)/chaperone(s). This may include staff, parents, and/or older teens.
- Depending on library policy:
  - Create sign-up list.
  - Distribute permission forms or contact parents of participants.

- Acknowledges Orth, "I did call each parent beforehand to let them know about the pick-up/drop-off time/place, and give details."

Day of
- Prep the library. This may include flag-hiding, object-obfuscating, placement of targets, and/or staging a table with name tags.
- Set a neutral area for teens to store snacks or take breaks. The area also serves as a quiet area for young people with Asperger's syndrome.

Immediately Prior
- Stage the table with name tags.
- To prevent theft, provide participants with a fifteen-minute window prior to the event to label their gear (including darts).
- Conduct a weapons inspection (30 minutes, may overlap with gear-labeling window).
  - "The captains looked over each gun for dangerous modifications, and to make sure only foam bullets were in use," Orth recalls.
- Brief the chaperones about their duties and the rules.
  - Identify territory covered by each chaperone.
  - In case of incident, request that chaperones send the floor captain to notify the teen librarian, who will be roaming.
- Form teams.
  - Review rules with participants.

After
- Allow 30 minutes at end for bullet retrieval.
- Clean up.
- Evaluate.
  - Pass out feedback sheets at end of program.
  - Discuss at next TAB meeting.
    - At Mount Laurel Library, Samantha Marker's teens evaluated the event, and suggested division by age or grade.

YA Involvement
- Teens create the rules.
- High school seniors may assist chaperones.
- YAs market via social networks, word-of-mouth, and blogs.
- Teens recruit chaperones.
- Blackwell's teens influenced her decision to stage the event. She remembers, "*The Forest of Hands and Teeth* and *Zombieland* were very popular with my teens at the time."

Partnerships

- A former TAB member returned to chaperone at Mount Laurel Library.
- A staff member whose son included the event in his birthday celebration also assisted with chaperoning at Mount Laurel Library.
- At Curtis Memorial Library, a participant's college-aged brother volunteered to video record the program using his personal equipment.

Feedback

Assessed via word-of-mouth and at the following TAB meeting.

Raves

"We had a turnout of around 30 teens, which was the largest we've ever had for a midweek program. And I'm still getting requests to do it again."–Tammy Blackwell

"I was anticipating 35 teens; we had 75! It's always rewarding to see new faces."–Samantha Marker

"Let's do this again!"–Teens of Curtis Memorial Library

"The teens love it and it is our most popular event."–Melissa Orth

Modifications

- The double tap looked cool in *Zombieland*, but flag-pulling is safer for library events.
- Teens suggest including a fast zombie. This hastened undead movement is based on the 2002 film *28 Days Later,* as well as the 2008 first-person shooter video game *Left 4 Dead*.
- Begin the game with more humans than zombies, so that humans are not overwhelmed by the competition.
- Separate competitors according to age (grades 6-9 versus grades 10-12). Older teens act as referees.
- Curtis Memorial Library offers a silent hide-and-go-seek game for individuals with Asperger's Syndrome.

Web Component

Using a wiki, Mount Laurel Library teens were able to view the game regulations and suggest rule changes for one month prior to the event.

Resources

"Zombies were just beginning their run as *the* thing in YA/pop culture when I decided to do this program," shares Blackwell. "The list was bouncing around several different zombie-related resources for various programs at the time, many of which I was able to take and use. For example, some members spoke of having the Zombie Squad come in to do a program at their library." Blackwell adapted this list advice for her library. "While there are no Zombie Squad members near us, I was able to use downloadable brochures from their website."

YAACers also consulted:

- http://humansvszombies.org/
- http://www.curtislibrary.com/teens/

Tips

"More Nerf guns," Blackwell says. "There can never be too many Nerf guns."

Mount Laurel Library Humans vs. Zombies game. Photograph by Samantha Marker

Lagniappe

Orth wonders, "[Is there] a polite way to hand out extra deodorant beforehand?" Consider contacting antiperspirant makers to request free samples to pass out at the door.

PDF, Rules, and Photo

Mount Laurel Library Facebook photos: http://www.facebook.com/home. php?#!/album.php?aid=472310&id=185794715136

**Mount Laurel
Library**

MOUNT LAUREL LIBRARY LOCKDOWN REGISTRATION FORM
Friday, October 29 8-10 PM
Grades 7-12

Name: _____

Full Address: _____

Home Telephone #: _____ Emergency #: _____

Grade: _____

Because of the physical nature of the Humans vs. Zombies event, we are requesting all participants have a permission form signed by a parent or legal guardian in order to participate

1. Participants will be granted permission to run at this lockdown. Participants do so at their own risk. The Mount Laurel Library will assume no responsibility for any injuries sustained in the course of the game.
2. Participants may bring their own Nerf dart guns for this event, but each participant is responsible for keeping track of his/her own darts. Labeling equipment with your name is highly advisable.
3. While the rules allow for Nerf darts to be shot at opponents, it is unacceptable to aim for a participant's head. Anyone believed to be violating this rule will be removed from the game, and may be asked to leave the lockdown.
4. Full rules of this event are available on our website: mtlaurel.lib.nj.us/teens/programs.html Please review them before the event.

I have read & understand these policies & I have informed my child of the policies, and he/she has full understanding of his/her responsibilities at the Library Lockdown Event.

Please return this form to the Mount Laurel Library. Teens will not be permitted to attend this event without parental consent. Contact Samantha Marker, Young Adult Librarian at the Mount Laurel Library for more information: (856) 234-7319 ext. 335 or smarker@mtlaurel.lib.nj.us

Parent/Guardian Signature: _____

The Mount Laurel Library is not responsible for lost or stolen articles while customers are in teen programs or facilities.

Rules and registration form courtesy of Samantha Marker

Humans vs. Zombies Lockdown Rules and Regulations

Equipment:
Humans will need: a bandanna   Optional: rolled socks, Nerf dart gun (subject to inspection)
Zombies do not require special equipment, but all participants will have the option to play both roles, so plan accordingly.
*Labeling all equipment with your name is highly recommended. The library is not responsible for lost, damaged, or stolen items.

Rules and Regulations:
All participants must have a permission slip signed by a parent or legal guardian to participate.

Participants will be divided into two teams: humans and zombies

The ratio of humans to zombies will be 1:5. This may be adjusted at the discretion of the Head Gamemaker, i.e. Sam.

Players must remain in the designated game area at all times.

Participants will take turns as both humans and zombies.

Humans will wear their bandannas tucked into the side of their pants (like a flag for flag football). When a zombie removes the flag, the human will be considered bitten and becomes a zombie. New zombies must abandon their equipment and can no longer aid the humans in achieving their mission. Humans may not grab or otherwise interfere with a zombie grabbing their flags. However, a zombie who is stunned in the process of grabbing a flag must release the flag immediately.

To combat the zombies, humans may shoot them with Nerf darts or throw sock grenades at them. If a zombie is hit with a dart or a grenade, it is stunned for a period of 15 seconds, during which time the zombie must lie down on the ground. While stunned, the zombie cannot bite a human.

Humans may not hit or shoot zombies in the head. Doing so will result in removal from the game and may result in removal from the lockdown. A zombie hit in the head will not be considered stunned.

Each game ends when the humans complete their mission successfully, or all humans have been turned to zombies.

Humans may run. Zombies may only walk unless they have been designated a fast zombie. Fast zombies will be determined at random and may not appear in every game.

These rules may be adapted at any time at the discretion of the Head Gamemaker.

Rules and registration form courtesy of Samantha Marker

Zombie Quickies

Since the rebirth of interest the genre, teen services professionals have generated a number of creative zombie-themed programming ideas.

Zombiefest

At the Lewis and Clark Library in Helena, Montana, Teen Services Librarian Pad McCraken offered teens the opportunity to dress in costume and parade through the downtown area on Halloween night. Prior to marching the streets, teens viewed zombie movies like *Army of Darkness* and chowed down on the living....errr...pizza. McCracken's young adults may be undead, but they ate up the lively event.

Zombie Muscial Chairs

Starkville Public Library YA Librarian Anna Ruhs recommends, "Play Zombie Musical Chairs. My teens played it last year at our Halloween party and they loved it. You place the chairs randomly about the room (not in a circle), and while the music is playing the kids have to walk around like zombies. No stalking chairs, and there was a prize for the best zombie walk as well as for the musical chairs winner. It was pretty hilarious."

Zombie Trivia

Kathleen Gruver of Burlington County Library System developed the following zombie trivia questions, which can be used in any number of games, including the circle game described in Chapter 2.

Question

- In zombie movies, where should one shoot to kill a zombie?

Answer

- Head

Question

- In *Army of Darkness*, what words does Ash distort, causing the zombie army to arise to life?

Answer

- "Klaatu barada nikto."

Question

- Which heavy metal band led by Rob Zombie was named for a 1932 horror film starring Bela Lugosi?

Answer

- *White Zombie*

Question

- Which AMC television series is based on a graphic novel series by Robert Kirkman, Tony Moore, and Charles Adlard?

Answer

- *The Walking Dead*

Question

- Who wrote *The Zombie Survival Guide* and *World War Z: An Oral History of the Zombie War*?

Answer

- Max Brooks

Question

- In George Romero's *Dawn of the Dead*, where do humans seek refuge from zombies?

Answer

- A shopping mall.

Question

- What is the title of the tower defense action videogame in which players situate various plant and fungus species—each with unique offensive or defensive capabilities—around a house to stop a horde of zombies from devouring residents' brains?

Answer

- Plants vs. Zombies

Question

- What city is overrun by zombies in the 2004 film *Shaun of the Dead*?

Answer

- London

Question

- What 1929 novel is credited with popularizing the word "zombie" in the English language?

Answer

- The Magic Island

Question

- In Stephen King's novel *Cell*, what sends out a mysterious signal that turns humans into zombies?

Answer

- Cell phones

Question

- In the Michael Jackson *Thriller* video, which famous horror actor raps at the end of the song?

Answer

- Vincent Price

Question

- On what gaming platform was the original *Resident Evil* game released in 1996?

Answer

- PlayStation

Question

- According to voodoo lore, what substance, if fed to a zombie, will make it recall that it is dead, then return to the grave?

Answer

- Salt

Question

- In *Harry Potter and the Half-Blood Prince*, what is the name for the dead humans who: (1) are reanimated by Dark Magic, and (2) try to keep Harry and Dumbledore from crossing the lake?

Answer

- Inferi

Question

- Which book is a mash-up of a famous Jane Austen novel and the tale of a zombie epidemic?

Answer

- *Pride and Prejudice and Zombies* by Seth Grahame-Smith

Question

- Which manga and anime series features high school students wandering through Japan as they try to survive a zombie pandemic?

Answer

- Highschool of the Dead

Question

- In the opening of the 1968 film *Night of the Living Dead*, what does one doomed brother say to his sister before being attacked by a zombie in the cemetery?

Answer

- "They're coming to get you, Barbara."

Question

- In which comic book series does a virus turn superheroes and civilians into zombies?

Answer

- Marvel Zombies

Question

- In *The Grim Adventures of Billy and Mandy*, who is the musical artist who sings "BRAINS?" ("BRAINS, BRAINS, I won't lie, I'll eat their brains 'til they're zombified! Sure they might think it's deranged. But they won't give it a thought. After I've eaten their brain.")

Answer

- Voltaire

Question

- Which teen book by Jonathan Maberry features zombie-killer brothers Tom and Benny Imura?

Answer

- Rot and Ruin

Question

- In Carrie Ryan's *The Forest of Hands and Teeth*, what are the infected zombies called?

Answer

- The Unconsecrated

Question

- What is the name of the zombie-themed live action game played on college campuses and libraries?

Answer

- Humans vs. Zombies

Zombie trivia courtesy of Kathleen Gruver, YA Librarian, Burlington County Library System, Westampton, New Jersey

3

Based on the Book: Literary Programs

Libraries celebrate literature with monograph-themed programming, including booktalks, book clubs, and author lectures. Young adult services professionals are introducing tweens and teens to this literary tradition by providing exciting programming that celebrates the written word with carefully selected food and drink, live action role-playing fun, lunchtime book clubs on school campuses, multimedia booktalks in the classroom, and much more. This chapter makes plain the details of programs described by YA-YAAC list contributors.

Has anyone ever done a library program where you make cardboard armor and do cardboard tube fighting? Or, if you've just done tube fighting (I know some of you have!), did you ask them to bring their own armor they made at home or did you go without protection?—Emily Fleischer, Brownsburg Public Library, Indiana

role-playing, n.

Pronunciation: Brit./ˈrəʊlˌpleɪɪŋ/, U.S./ˈroʊlˌpleɪɪŋ/

Etymology: < role *n.* + playing *n.* Compare role-player *n.*

Participation in a role-playing game; the playing of (a role in) such games.

1980 People 14 Jan. 67/2 Next comes role-playing. Adopting a mythic-sounding name, a player heavy with intelligence might choose to be a wizard.[1]

Description

Young adults are adjusting to newly developing physiques, alternately clear and pimpled complexions, and constantly fluctuating moods. It's no wonder that teens appreciate the escape of embodying a spunky anime heroine, brooding dreamer, or diabolical villain. Live action role-play, or LARP, allows players to become characters in a story that is dramatized in real life. Participants simulate events, compete, and achieve goals in accordance with game rules. Imagination is key in LARPing, and players often create costumes (though costuming isn't required). Like improvisational theater, inexpensive props may be used to inspire creativity. Well-known examples of live action role-play include mystery dinner games and historical reenactments.

Similar to Zombie Nerf Turf Wars, *Hunger Games* LARPing offers tweens and teens the opportunity to battle in the library. Participants assemble and decorate cardboard armor and swords, then attack one another. At the Glendale Public Library in Arizona, young adults were also tasked with finding concealed food and water cards.

Describing the Marshall County Public Library program, Young Adult Librarian Tammy Blackwell posts, "Our war was the grand finale of a Ren Faire. I had allotted about 30 minutes, but it only took about 10 (or even less) for one team to pretty much slaughter the other. Still, it was tons of fun and they're still talking about it eight months later." She continues, "We didn't have armor, but I did have some heavily enforced rules: No hitting someone above the shoulders and you must swing from the elbows. Since the tubes didn't break as easily, our game was more like LARP-ing. Touch a person's arm or leg and they lose the ability to use that limb. To kill, you must touch a person's torso. If your sword breaks (which did happen when swords where whacked together), then you're out. I posted the rules everywhere around the site and repeated them several times before the game began and we ended up not having any issues whatsoever."

Steps
Before

- Refer to Nerf Turf Wars/Humans vs. Zombies program for detailed instructions regarding running live action role-playing games.

---

1. "role-playing, n." OED Online. June 2011. Oxford University Press. http://www.oed.com/view/Entry/246441 (accessed September 10, 2011).

- Prepare food and water cards.

Immediately Prior
- Hide food and water cards throughout library.

During
- Divide participants into teams.
- Each team creates armor, shields, and swords from cardboard using provided supplies.
- Teams battle!
- When the sword (cardboard tube) is broken, that team member is out of the game, but can still hunt for food and water cards in the library to aid team members.
- Within 30 minutes, all surviving members must have both water and food rations. If not, that team member is pronounced dead. Young Adult Librarian Anna Ruhs shares, "'Dead' people stayed where they died until the round was over, and were not allowed to be stepped on. This worked really well, no one got injured, and we had a good time."

After
- Clean up the library with assistance from teen volunteers.

Cost
- Staff time
  - "Very staff and labor intensive," is a caveat noted by Jenson-Benjamin.
- Supply cost varies, $0-$300

Supplies
- Food and water cards
- Scissors
- Packing tape
- Markers
- Cardboard tubes and boxes
  - YAACers traded advice regarding procurement of cardboard tubes.
    - Blackwell explains, "I ended up having to order tubes from a company that sold packing supplies. I got the most lightweight thing they offered, but it was still a little stronger than the typical wrapping paper center."

- "Cardboard tubes can be hard to find," agrees Val Fisher of Milford, Connecticut. "I am always collecting them."

Program Type

Active

Duration

Varies, up to 3 hours

Planning Time

Varies, 3-8 hours

Marketing

Some of the YA-YAAC posters to this discussion promoted their events in library flyers.

Partnerships

"Consider inviting your local sport fencing club! We invited ours and they gave a wonderful demo, and brought equipment for teens to try their hand at the sport, which is much closer to the movie 'moves,'" recommends Richmond Memorial Library Youth Services Assistant Kelly March.

Young Adult Librarian Sandy Moltz comments, "Last year, our library had the local chapter of the Society for Creative Anachronism come and do a jousting and medieval dancing presentation." Moltz explains that the Society for Creative Anachronism "considers these visits a mission of the organization, so there is no charge." The kids jousted on the lawn next to the library before going inside for the dancing. Moltz says, "Everyone had a blast. Many of the kids have asked when I'm going to have them back again."

Raves

- "It was a really fun night!" relishes Jenson-Benjamin.
- Posting from the United Kingdom, Dana Cohlmeyer, a graduate student at University of Edinburgh, gushes, "I LOVED my jousting activity this summer (and so did the kids!)"

Modifications

- Cohlmeyer offers an alternative jousting option: "We decorated shields I bought from Oriental Trading [and] taped them to the rolling chairs in our meeting room. We paired [the teens] up and had them go in pairs, [giving] each jouster a pool noodle. We had 'heralding trumpets' on the iPod. We laughed our butts off as each pair went for each other."

- Teen Librarian Kristie Revicki shares, "The pool noodle jousts at the Ren Faire we had at the library were definitely a hit this summer! We ordered adult sized hop-along balls to use as horses. This added an extra element of instability." The winner "was either the only person to stay on their bouncy ball, or they got the tip of their pool noodle onto their opponent's chest first."
- Campbell County Public Library Youth Services Librarian Susan Knesel offers another battle option: "We made jousting circles with masking tape. When they stepped out, they lost."

Web Component

- Need inspiration? Check out the video posted by Glendale Public Library: http://youtu.be/MYEN3rHaaoA

Suggested shopping site: http://www.jumpingballs.com/categories/Balls/ Jumping-Balls/Hoppity-Hop-Balls-for-Ages-13-to-Adult/

PROGRAM

Twihards Tweaking out @ Your Twibrary

Confession time," admits a YAACer, "I only read the first one and half of the second [Twilight novels]." Entreating colleagues, our guilt-ridden teen services librarian adds, "I am scrambling for party ideas!

Twilight and New Moon are extremely faithful adaptations of Meyer's novels, something deeply satisfying to Twihards, as fans of Meyer's saga are called, and vexing to film critics writing for major publications.[2]—Encyclopedia of the Vampire: The Living Dead in Myth, Legend, and Popular Culture

Tweaks: Twilight freaks[3]

2. Joshi, S. T. 2011. *Encyclopedia of the Vampire: The Living Dead in Myth, Legend, and Popular Culture* (p. 334). ABC-CLIO, eBook Collection, EBSCOhost (accessed September 18, 2011).
3. Konjicanin, Anja. "Robert Pattinson, Kristen Stewart, Taylor Lautner and Twilight crew generate new fan slang in Squamish." Posted April 15, 2011. *The Vancouver Observer* (accessed September 10, 2011).

Description

Over the years, twilingual YAACers have posted ideas for colleagues undertaking frighteningly fabulous fêtes in celebration of the beloved vampire series by Stephenie Meyer. *Twilight* programs remain consistently popular with tweens and teens—count on a crowd when staging an event for twihard fans.

Ac-Twi-vities

- Twibrarians are in agreement that purchasing parlor games ($10-$20) is a valuable timesaver. "I did a Google search for *Twilight* parties," Rebecca Baldwin divulges. "The only game idea I liked was pin the tail on the werewolf. I am investing in a *Twilight* Scene It? game."

- At Palo Alto City Library, actors from the local children's theater will greet *Breaking Dawn* partygoers. The performers will be in character as Bella, Edward, and Jacob. "I don't think we'll be having food," jokes Librarian Cheryl Lee. "Since vampires don't eat."

- "Marble magnets were a popular craft at *Twilight* parties I've done," reflects Teen Librarian Karl Siewart. "Your basic marble magnet is a sandwich made of a round magnet, a picture, and a flat 'marble.' It's all glued together with clear adhesive, and the marble acts as a magnifier for the picture. You can use a second magnet to turn them into little badges. I've had great luck with E6000, a readily available craft adhesive. Some of my magnets are two years old, and they haven't yellowed." Siewart suggests, "Invest in a ½" paper punch…it makes everything much faster. Before the day of the movie, take some cardstock or light cardboard [and] make a bunch of viewfinders by cutting out squares and punching ½" holes in them. These allow the teens to visualize exactly how much of Edward's face is going to show."

- Young Adult Services and Reference Librarian Katie Spofford recommends that twihards compete in a Name Bella's Child contest. "It should be easy to come up with a better name than Renesmee!"

- "Our Friends of the Library provides funds for our programming," discloses Teen Services Librarian Christina Getrost. The Stow-Munroe Falls Public Library distributes copies of titles like *Breaking Dawn* "as door prizes at their respective release parties."

- "Our friends group bought life-sized cardboard cutouts of Bella, Jacob, and Edward, and during the evening people could get their pictures taken with them," pipes in Youth Services Librarian Ami Segna. The backdrop featured quotes from the books on black paper with red glitter, stapled to the back wall. She adds, "I used my digital camera and they had to leave an e-mail address, so the pictures didn't cost a cent. We had a trivia contest, top three winners to receive one of the figures, and I told them they had to turn it in before they left." Be warned, twibrarians; this innocent competition may turn deadly. "They took me so seriously, when the fire alarm went off suddenly, nobody would move from the room! (False alarm, fortunately)."

- In Springfield, Missouri, Sarah Bean Thompson's young adults were treated to an *Eclipse* prom. "We even hired a DJ."
- Blogger Whitney posts to the Youth Services Corner site, "A librarian on the YA-YAAC list suggested a 'Drive like a Cullen' race course with cheap remote control cars from Wal-Mart and others suggested a vampires vs. werewolves tug-of-war."[4]
- Teen Librarian Cindy Simerlink suggests pinning *Twilight* character names to participants' backs. Explains Simerlink, "They have to ask people yes or no questions to figure out who they have." She hints to party planners, "Turn to the index [of *Breaking Dawn*] and include all the vampires that didn't show up until then!"
  - Herriman Public Library's Patricia Foster adds, "To get a longer list of names, you can also include the models of the cars they drive."

Steps
Before
Be prepared! Electri-twi-ed tweens and teens will swiftly colonize at the library for any vamped-up event.
- Assign jobs to teen volunteers, e.g., craft preparation, creating name tags, etc.
- Promote the event via signage, social networks (online or in-person), and intercom announcements at local schools.

Day of
- Set up event area. If using Scene It?, insert the game DVD and conduct a test run (using a television and DVD player).

Immediately Prior
- If using standees, get the camera and backdrop ready for action.

After
- To make the images available to participants, post, email, or print pictures of fanpires with standees.

Cost

$0-$75

Program Type

Active

Duration

1-3 hours (suggested)

Planning Time

3-8 hours

Marketing

- "What about a themed tree?" Morton Grove Public Library's Christina Thurairatnam remembers, "One library I visited has a contest every year for people to decorate Christmas trees. One group did a *Twilight* tree using ornaments made of pictures of book covers, red-tipped white flowers, etc." A *Twilight* tree serves as a unique promotional tool for book-related programming—Christmas present, past, *or* future.

YA Involvement

- Enlist young adult volunteers to assist with preparing the party space.

Teen Services Librarian II Merideth Jenson-Benjamin says, "We bit the bullet and bought the *Twilight* Scene It? Deluxe Edition for $12. It was worth it for us to spend the money, rather than eat up staff time writing trivia questions. Particularly since none of us are big fans of the series."

- If a *Twilight* board game is available, assign a teen volunteer to the task of learning the rules and acting as moderator.
  - The game moderator's knowledge will ease the learning curve of the group, thus helping the event progress smoothly.
  - Ask a teen to prepare to act as stand-in moderator.

If teen volunteers are delegated the job of cleaning up after the event, be assured that (unless distracted) these energetic helpers will make quick work of the task.

Teen volunteers can help create a display to promote vampiric events! Photograph by Monique Delatte Starkey

Photograph by Monique Delatte Starkey

Partnerships

- "For the *Twilight* movie releases," offers Collection and Programming Specialist Librarian Amy Arey, "we've teamed up with the local movie theater to set up a table to promote the library."
- Even twiguys will appreciate a sugary homage to the series. Consider coordinating with a local bakery to request the donation of vampire-themed treats. Teen Librarian Cindy Simerlink enthuses, "Vampire cupcakes—these are AWESOME!"

Web Component

- Siewart posts, "You can find a lot of tutorials online. My favorite is at NotMartha": http://www.notmartha.org/tomake/marble-magnets/
- Segna shares the following blog link: http://3tnar.blogspot.com/2009/11/new-moon-party.html.
- Information Professional Andrea Graham offers this tutorial: http://www.4yablog.com/2010/05/celebrate-eclipse-with-vampire-cupcakes.html

Lagniappe

Feeling dirty about promoting an event for a book that is arguably not well-written? Consider the advice of Sarah Dentan, Branch Services Manager/Youth Services, Sacramento Public Library: "Believe me, I feel the Bieber-cringe; heck, I feel the *Twilight*-cringe. But the fact of the matter is, kids need connection—with each other and with safe adults—and those events create the space for those things to happen. In the right hands, those events can become what a colleague calls 'stealth book clubs,' and provide a bridge to other material that some of us might consider, well, better. They also validate kids' tastes—while I will share my critique of *Twilight* with anyone who asks, and suggest books I think are better examples of the genre, I want to value and validate kids, and that means being excited (or at least, letting THEM be excited) about what they're excited about."

<table>
<tr><td>PROGRAM</td></tr>
<tr><td>*Harry Potter Party*</td></tr>
</table>

Harry Potter Quickie

*A couple of months ago, I got really into Harry Potter. It's really good!" stand-up comic Kumail Nanjiani jokes. "But I resisted for years 'cause I was like, 'If that many people like it, how good could it be?' Pretty...good! It's pretty...good! From a vicarious standpoint, you know? 'Cause it's this kid, he transfers, and then his life is completely different. And, like, I transferred in high school and it was awful. People disliked me just 'cause I was new. Like on Valentine's Day, these [expletive deleted] sent a girl a bouquet with my name on them. And, then, a bird [expletive deleted] on my head, **and I hid in the library all day**. That is a true story. None of that is lies.[5]*

Description

Libraries have been planning Harry Potter *soirées since the nineties, so ideas posted to the list have been honed to perfection.*

Cornucopia of YAACers HP fête ideas:

- Director of Youth Services Anna Brannin reveals that her library will "include a birthday card for Harry that everyone will sign, [and] a booth where we draw a lightning bolt on their forehead and give them a pair of Harry glasses." Also planned is "wand-making, a photo op (we ordered a Harry Potter broom and made a Golden Snitch for them to pretend to catch!), and Honeydukes. They have to answer a trivia question to get a bag of candy. I'm making a long list of trivia questions for any teens to answer. I'll draw three entries that have every question right for a prize." Hancock County Library will also offer young adults the chance to

---

5. John Oliver's New York Stand-Up Show. Comedy Central. April 28, 2011. Episode 12, minute 13.

test their knowledge with the Harry Potter Scene It? game, which Brannin ordered online. She writes, "It's only $30 right now and has clips/trivia from all EIGHT movies! That will be playing on our projector screen on party mode. We're not having a costume contest, but anyone that comes in costume gets an extra...prize."

- Tuning in from Canada, Teen Services Librarian Teresa Gawman and Children's and Adult Fiction Assistant Andrea Adair Tippins of Whitby Public Library contribute their crowd-pleaser:
  1. Forming Play-Doh in a transfiguration challenge.
     - According to Gawman, "One kid transfigured while the others had to guess what it is." She awards the prize (Horcrux) "based on what house won each game/event. The goal was to get as many as possible."
     - Like Brannin, Gawman and Adair also "gave out treat bags from Honeydukes."
  2. Playing the game Who Am I? "Kids get a [character's] name taped to their back, and they have to guess who they are." (YAACers adapt this game for numerous thematic events.)
  3. Sorting the kids into the four different houses.
  4. Competing in Harry Potter *Jeopardy!* and Harry Potter trivia.
  5. Creating potions. (Gawman suggests that event planners fill a tumbler with water, then add a few tablespoons of vegetable oil and a pinch of kosher salt. "Looks like a lava lamp.")
  6. Pinning the tail on Dudley.
  7. Making a Golden Snitch.
- Young Adult Librarian Evan Day shares, "We're holding a two-day marathon of the movies."
- Angela Germany posts to the YALSA blog:
  - Use your imagination to create and serve:
    - Cauldron cakes (cupcakes with neon green icing, molten lava cake with neon-colored filling, etc.)
    - Pumpkin juice (Tang)
    - Butter beer (apple cider or root beer)
- Germany also passes along a passive programming option: "Create handouts for teens to complete. Award cheap silly prizes or candy bars for teens who participate."
- North Branch Summit County Library Director Janet Good outlines her programming activity:
  - We played a game at a Harry Potter party where I gave each kid a square of cardboard about 6" by 6". I had them put the cardboard on top of their heads, and draw Harry Potter's face in this order:

1. Draw an oval for his face.
2. Draw hair on his head
3. Draw his mouth.
4. Draw his ears.
5. Draw his eyes.
6. Draw his nose.
7. Draw the lightning scar on his forehead.

She confirms, "Of course, the object is to keep the cardboard on top of your head without looking at it the whole time. We had some hilarious results."

Has anyone done a Superman program? I'm blanking!

PROGRAM

Superman Celebration

Description

YAACers offer several program suggestions including upcycling, taking photographs with a Superman backdrop, and a stenciling project.

Activity 1
Upcycle Superman Comics

upcycle

Pronunciation: /ˈʌpsʌɪk(ə)l/ verb

reuse (discarded objects or material) in such a way as to create a product of higher quality or value than the original: the opportunity to upcycle trash, or turn it into new products, was vast (as adjective upcycled) upcyled furniture[6]

Upcycle to teach teens to reinvent that most sacred of parchment—touched by the muses and appropriately stamped with library markings to identify place and time. Since well-loved comic books are often the first library materials to dilapidate, they are great fodder for an upcycling project. Regular list poster and eBuzzing blogger Andrea Graham urges YA program planners to découpage a Superman comic book wallet, cuff, earrings, or coasters. Graham suggests checking out the 4ya blog for links to video instructions and samples: http://www.4yablog.com/2011/04/super-comic-book-upcycle-projects.html. At La Verne Library, Shanda Nelson's

---

6. "upcycle, v.". Oxford Dictionaries. April 2010. Oxford University Press. http://oxforddictionaries.com/definition/upcycle (accessed July 21, 2011).

YAs absolutely *lurve* the découpaging of wood block shapes, which may be purchased for $1 apiece at craft stores.

Activity 2
Fun Photo Backgrounds

Create a backdrop of clouds against an azure sky, or construct a phone booth on a city street. (Or assign the task to artistic teen volunteers.) Then, proposes Karl Siewart of Tulsa Library, turn on a fan and rotate the set or camera sideways. Challenge teens to assume their boldest Superman pose. Snap pictures and print at least one photo for each teen.

Activity 3
"S" Logo Stenciling

Beth Dailey Kenneth of Highland Branch Library recommends cutting an "S" logo from cardboard for use as a stencil to upcycle teens' T-shirts, jeans, pillowcases, and backpacks. The Memphis librarian cautions, "Just remember to put cardboard between the layers to stop the stencil from bleeding!" For a shape that slips perfectly into a tee, snag the sleeves from the unwanted records that have been collecting dust in the Friends of the Library book sale, hints La Puente Library Artist-in-Residence Blanca Aranda.

Supplies

Upcycling: comic books (donated, deselected, or newly purchased), paper rolls from the interior of packing tape, heavy posterboard, Mod Podge or white glue, wood blocks/shapes from craft stores
Backdrops: camera, cape, fan, sport coat, Clark Kent glasses, foam board, markers (or paint and paintbrushes)
Stenciling: cardboard, scissors, sponges, water cups, paintbrushes, fabric paint or fabric marker pens, iron, ironing board, record sleeves

Cost

Varies according to materials on hand, ranges from $0-$75

Program Type

Comic book-themed

Duration

1-3 hours

Planning Time

Varies depending on marketing, preparation assistance, and materials already on hand. Expect 2-8 hours of prep.

YA Involvement

Teen volunteers can assist with the prep work, e.g., making backdrops or selecting magazine pages for collages.

Lagniappe

Teen Services Librarian Heidi Andres of Cuyahoga County Public Library recommends visiting the following sites:

- http://www.supermanhomepage.com/inter-action/inter-action. php?topic=kids-craft1
- http://www.cubeecraft.com/cubee/superman
- http://www.flickr.com/photos/bombusdesign/2163463019/
- http://fc06.deviantart.net/fs42/f/2009/113/3/7/Perler_Superman_necklace_by_FatalJapan.jpg

Marketing

Post signs, distribute fliers, ask teens to spread the word, and consider asking the library staff to wear Superman T-shirts on the day of the event.

Partnerships

Work with a local comic book shop to procure freebies or graphic novels for découpage.

Feedback

Pass out comment forms to gauge teen enjoyment of the program. Reviews of the preceding programs by Los Angeles teens:

- "More painting projects."—M. Lopez, 11th grade
- "Keep making more fun projects."—R. Martinez, 12th grade

Photos

Spread Mod Podge with a paintbrush to add shine, or prior to applying comic book images. Spread more Mod Podge after images have been applied. (See below for final product samples.) Photograph by Adriana Caratachea

Teen découpage projects. Photograph by Monique Delatte Starkey

Pin the [insert object] on the [insert character]

Harry Potter Quickie 2

Who else is having a Harry Potter party of sorts next week? We are! And I need some help! Kids always love games in the style of Pin the Tail on the Donkey (I've done pin the feather on the turkey for Thanksgiving, pin the red nose on Rudolph for Christmas, etc.), and I was thinking of having a pin the glasses on Harry-style game, but the thought of cutting out 50ish pairs of glasses is not fun. And, I don't think I'd do any justice to Harry when sketching him out. Can anyone think of another type of game that is…connected to the series, and would be easier to execute? Happy Harry Potter Week!—Director of Youth Services Anna Brannin, Hancock County Library System

Suggestions

- Foothills Branch Library Teen Librarian II Kristin Fletcher-Spear recalls, "Our first HP party for kids had **pin the tail on Dudley**. One of our children's librarians drew a Dudley figure."
- "**Pin a wand or lightning bolt scar on Harry**?" offers Middleburg Heights Branch Library Teen Services Librarian Heidi Andres.
  - "I would be careful," cautions Suffern Free Library's Kristie Revicki of the Pin the Wand on the Harry game, "if you are anticipating middle school boys." She recollects, "One of the benefits of having no female friends throughout middle school is that now I can see all the potential bad innuendos a 12-year-old boy might."
- "**Pin the bow on Umbridge**!" joins in Children's Librarian Frances Veit of Buckham Memorial Library. "You could also **draw the scar on Harry**. If you laminate or cover a picture of him, you just need a dry erase marker."

Pin the [insert object] on the [insert character]:
Random

- "Pin the tail variations (can they **pin something funny on a picture of you**?)" is a recommendation attributed to Ami Segna by Erin Marsh.
- A humorous tail-pinning game suggestion comes from Cumberland County Public Library Youth Services Librarian Maggie Hargrave, "**Pin the abs on the Jacob**. I have the Taylor Lautner Read poster, and I was going to make some paper abs that my teens could stick on him."
- Andres adds, "**Pin the slushie on the Glee club member**?"

4

Educational and Technological Programs

Sharing learning opportunities with teens is among the most rewarding aspects of working with young people. In this chapter, librarians share their most successful educational and technological programs.

"Take a study break and go outside, but don't forget to look up. This app will help you track your place in this world with the constellations."[1]—"Top 10 Back-to-School Apps"

PROGRAM

Star Walk

Description

"Star Walk is splendid. You can use this app on the iPhone, 4th-generation iPod, and the iPad," writes Raymond Shubinski for Astronomy. "Point your device at the sky, and Star Walk will display what's in that area: constellations, stars, and planets."[2]

---

1. "Top 10 Back-to-School Apps." 2011. *Inventors' Digest* 27, no. 9: 26. MasterFILE Premier, EBSCOhost (accessed September 26, 2011).
2. Shubinski, Raymond. 2011. "There's an astro app for that." *Astronomy* 39, no. 8: 58. MasterFILE Premier, EBSCOhost (accessed September 27, 2011).

"Curtis Memorial has 10 iPads for staff use with the public," explains Teen Librarian Melissa Orth. Her fun tech program includes "using the Star Walk app on iPads to lead teens and young adults in viewing the constellations of the winter and summer night sky, with guidance from a docent from a local planetarium. Our teens love using the iPad and the Star Walk app is fun and easy to use."

Supplies

iPads loaded with Star Walk app

Steps

Before

- Market the event, working with middle or high school science teachers to award extra credit to participants.
- Coordinate with a local planetarium to book a docent to lead the walk. "We invited a docent volunteer from the local planetarium to walk us through the night sky," says Orth. "She arrived with a laser pointer and a plethora of stories."

Week of

- Download the Star Walk app to iPads. Orth shares, "To prep the iPads for public use, we moved all other apps to folders on the dock, so only the Star Walk app showed."

During

- Docent leads the event, describing the night sky for attendees.

After

- Check iPads back in.
- Offer comment forms to participants.

Cost

- $5, if library owns iPads.
  - "If your library already has iPads for use, the app is $5," details Orth. "If multiple iPads are synced to the same iTunes account, this could be an inexpensive program. Once the materials are purchased, the event costs nothing to subsequently host. The docent volunteered her time."
  - Other cost-saving solutions include:

- Plan for attendees to share library iPads.
- Invite participants to bring their own e-device with the app loaded.
- Staff time (Orth had one assistant.)

Program Type
- Active
- Fun for tweens, teens, and new adults (Orth defines new adults as 20- to 25-year-olds.)

Duration
30-60 minutes

Planning Time
1-3 hours

Marketing
- The Star Walk is a biannual opportunity for Curtis Memorial to promote the library iPads. Says Orth, "The event showed the community that we have iPads, and know how to use them in fun ways."
- "Lorri Centineo returns to help identify constellations," proclaims library newsletter *Curtis News*, "and talk about the mythology behind their names."[3]

Feedback
Orth says, "We orally surveyed the attendees at the close of the program."

YA Involvement
Star Walks attract new blood. Declares Orth, "We had young adults attend who had never come to the library!"

Partnerships
Curtis Memorial Library collaborated with both the University of Southern Maine Southworth Planetarium and Cornerstones of Science. Orth explains, "Partnering with the planetarium was perfect since they provided a knowledgeable docent who was also a great storyteller. It fit the

Cornerstones of Science Foundation's initiative to provide science-based programming in an accessible and fun way." In addition to donated time and expertise, Orth received Cornerstones of Science funding, which the library used to purchase the Star Walk app that had been mentioned in *School Library Journal*.

Raves

"We were really pleased to have reached the young adult crowd," says Orth.

Tips

1. Don warm apparel in anticipation of nighttime temperatures.
2. "Spend more time inside first to allow patrons to get familiar with the app," stresses Orth.

Accommodations

- "We had one iPad set up in voice mode and large type for a developmentally disabled attendee."
- Orth adds, "Another attendee with Asperger's Syndrome needed no accommodations, but was extremely happy that the program did not require much personal interaction."

Web Component

- http://www.curtislibrary.com/programs-events/cornerstones-of-science-2/
- https://www.facebook.com/CMLteens

Lagniappe

- Consider offering the program as an off-site event. Curtis Memorial planned a summer Star Walk at a local farm where participants enjoyed a clear view of the night sky.

PROGRAM

Project: Anime Fest

anime, n.[3]

Pronunciation: Brit. /ˈanɪmeɪ/ , U.S. /ˈænəmeɪ/
Etymology: < Japanese anime animation (1970 or earlier), shortened < animēshon

---

3. "NOOK, STARS & MARS." 2011. *Curtis News* 22, no. 3: 8.

A genre of Japanese or Japanese-style animated film or television entertainment, characterized by a distinctive visual style involving stylized action sequences and usually featuring characters with distinctive large, staring eyes, and typically having a science-fiction or fantasy theme, sometimes including violent or sexually explicit material; a film or television programme of this genre.[4]

2001 ON 5 Feb. 81/1 The setting is an anime standard: a dreary, postindustrial Tokyo-type city.

Description

Teen Services Assistant Heather Price of Spartanburg County Public Libraries (SCPL) writes, "Anime Fest consisted of four main activities: an hour-long Skype session with manga artist Svetlana Chmakova; a brief dance session in which teens could learn and dance the Caramell Dance, Caipirinha, and Danjo (all dances inspired by anime-related YouTube memes); a cosplay contest (with two prizes awarded, one audience-selected, one judge-selected); and an anime screening."

Steps

Before

- Preregister the participants.
- Book the presenters.
  - The SCPL event included VOIP. Shares Price, "Since many of my teens are interested in becoming manga artists, I knew that I definitely wanted to either bring in a manga artist or Skype with one. This would be my main event, so I made a list of English-speaking manga artists." She then worked her way down the list until finding one suitable for the event.
  - Promote the event.
- Select an anime flick.
- Determine the order of events. Says Price:

  "Once I had the speaker settled, I proceeded to plan out the events that would follow it, starting with a high-energy event that would allow the teens to work off their fidgets (the meme dances), proceeding with a calmer event (the cosplay contest),

---

4. "anime, n.3". OED Online. June 2012. Oxford University Press. http://www.oed.com/view/Entry/248729?rskey=6QGqEG&result=3&isAdvanced=false (accessed August 7, 2012).

and finally ending on one that allowed for a fair amount of noise and enthusiasm (anime screenings in our club always tend to be energetic ones)."

Immediately Prior

- Log into the Skype session.
- Prepare the room for dance class.
- Clear an area for cosplay contest.
- Set up the anime film.

Program

- Cosplay
  - Library event planners review the costumes, then "judge on detail (that is, the closeness of the costume to the original character's costume), craftsmanship (the general quality of the costume, with handmade costumes taking higher points values than store-bought costumes), and presentation (how well the character, in character, was presented to the judges)." Price adds, "We consider general enthusiasm, rather than accuracy, since not all of the judges were entirely familiar with individual anime characters."

Cost

- *Varies from $100-$250*
- *Staff time (3 individuals planned/assisted)*

Program Type

- Passive
- Planned for *12-19-year-olds*

Planning Time

6-10 hours

Alternatives and Inspiration

"I visit anime conventions semi-frequently, so I tried to adapt events that I observed at these conventions to the library scale," Price explains. "Some events that I considered included anime-themed cosplay panels such as 'Ask an Anime Character' (wherein cosplayers accept questions from audience members and answer them in character), and games such as Cosplay

Chess (where cosplayers play a game of human chess, acting out short battle scenes when one 'piece' takes another)." She adds, "I also did simple Google searches to see what libraries that had conducted similar programs and what they did at these programs."

Building Local Connections

The library purchased gift cards from a local comic shop to give away as prizes.

Tips

"I would either cut the anime screening at the end or otherwise make sure that a highly anticipated new release was to be shown," says Price. "The teens enjoyed the anime that they selected (Ouran High School Host Club), but since it was an older release (though popular), it rendered the very end of the program somewhat anticlimactic."

Raves

"The program's attendance numbers rank in our highest for the summer," says Price. "The Skype session with Svetlana Chmakova was great, content-wise, though there were some minor trip-ups with Skype itself due to a lagging Internet connection (nothing significant, though). Svetlana herself was excellent to work with, too, in terms of making sure the session went as smoothly as possible. The meme dances and cosplay contest were also popular among the teens."

Lagniappe

Price states, "Project: Anime is one of our most popular monthly programs. In this program, teens complete an anime-related activity (usually a craft or food sampling) before watching any of a selection of three offered anime. Since summertime allows for more extravagant programs, we wanted to do something a bit more complex, involving more than a craft and anime screening. Project: Anime Fest is what resulted."

Cosplay Contest

GALLACON 2009

Cosplay Contest Judging Information

Criteria:

- **Detail of costume**—How well the costume conforms to the character.
- **Effort**—How much time and work went into the costume.
- **Presentation**—How well the contestant presents their character to the judges.

Points:

- Each judge can award up to 20 points to a contestant. Totals will be determined at the end of the judging period.
- Judges may choose to award a contestant points in the following manner:
  1. Up to 5 points for detail of costume
  2. Up to 10 points for effort
  3. Up to 5 points for presentation

Cosplay contest judging information courtesy of Suzanne Robinson and Nashville Public Library

GALLACON 2009
Cosplay Contest Sample Questions

1. What is the name of the character you are portraying?

2. Is this an actual character or a character that you developed?
   _____ Actual   _____ Self-developed

3. Do you have a picture of your character? (Ask if reference photo is not with entry.)

4. From what series or title is your character?

5. What does your character do?

6. Is your character a hero, a villain, or a regular person?

7. Does he/she have any special powers or abilities?

8. Why did you choose this character for your entry in the contest?

9. How much of your costume did you make yourself?

10. If you had help, how much of the work did your helper do?

Cosplay contest sample questions courtesy of Suzanne Robinson and Nashville Public Library

Rules & Guidelines

Submission Deadline: Tuesday, October 20, 2009 by 8:00 p.m.

Judging begins promptly at 5:30 pm. Prizes will be awarded following the judging.

Inglewood Branch Library

Prizes are as follows:

We will crown three winners: 1st Place, 1st Runner-Up, and 1st Honorable Mention.

Winners will receive Party City gift cards.

Every entrant will receive a certificate of participation.

Contest Guidelines:

Contest is open to persons ages 12-18.

You must have a Nashville Public Library card in good standing to enter. (If you don't have a library card—what are you waiting for? Sign up!)

Costumes must relate to anime, manga, video game, or comic book characters.

Additional weight will be given to costumes that are homemade rather than purchased. Props, wigs, and shoes may be homemade or purchased as long as they comply with contest rules.

Costumes must be suitable for a PG audience. No bathing suits, revealing outfits, or other clothing determined inappropriate by Gallacon organizers will be permitted.

Props must be made of plastic or flexible material. No metal or wooden props may be used. NO weapons may be brought onto library property. This is a violation of library policy and will result in immediate suspension of library privileges.

No flash powder, confetti, silly string, or similar material may be used during the contest.

Contestants must provide a reference picture of your character for the judges. Reference pictures may be printed from the Internet, a book, film cover, or any other source.

Your completed entry form, including reference picture, must be dropped off at any Nashville Public Library location by 5:30 p.m., Monday, October 19, 2009.

Costumes will be judged on detail (how close the costume is to the actual character); effort (how much time and work went into your costume); and presentation (how well you present your character to the judges).

For more information about this contest, please contact Suzanne Robinson at 862-5866.

Cosplay Contest
Entry Form

Name: _____

Grade: _____ Age: _____ Phone number: _____

Library card barcode _____

Address: _____

Character—Provide the name of the character you will be portraying and the anime/manga/game that they are from: _____

Character Description—Provide a brief overview of your character:

Prop(s) and Prop Materials—List the props that will be included as part of your costume: _____

Costume Preparation—How much time did you spend preparing your costume: _____

I give my permission for the Library to publish my photo in costume on the Library's website.

Signature: _____

Date: _____

(co-signing Parent or Guardian)_____

Cosplay contest information and flyer courtesy of Suzanne Robinson and Nashville Public Library

Bingo and Library Information Session

Bingo Quickie

I am new to my position and was just approached by a group that works with special needs teen girls about doing a small program for them at the library," says Beachwood Branch Library Teen Services Librarian Amy Dreger. *"They are working on life skills and are going to be going over how to act in and use a library. They are coming in two weeks for a tour and then a brief program where I will go over the library rules with them."* The Cuyahoga County Library librarian explains, *"I offered to jazz it up a little with a bingo game to hold their interest. I thought I could discuss a rule and then have a little picture symbol that goes with it. This sounds a bit juvenile, but I am trying to keep in mind that these are special needs kids on varying levels of ability…and who doesn't love a rousing game of bingo?"* She inquires, *"Does anyone have any other suggestions or just any tips in general for working with this population?"*

Description

Gloria Cumpston of Public Library of Enid and Garfield County replies, "I am a retired special education teacher, now a teen librarian. The bingo idea is perfect. Keep the symbols simple and distinctive, different colors, shapes, etc., so that they are not easily confused. Don't try to present too much information at one meeting. Hit the basics, and repeat them often in your presentation. Acting out the behavior is much better than just describing it." Cumpston recommends, "Don't get too wordy or offer too much explanation that causes overload. Keep it simple. You might make a poster of the symbols, and what they stand for, so that the students can refer to it."

5

Mindless Youth Indulgence: Pop Culture Programs

Remaining *au courant* can be helpful for librarians who serve young adults, demonstrating an interest in the culture that influences the way that teens dress, the music with which they identify, and the paperbacks that they dog-ear and pass among friends. Librarians bring an appreciation of the timeless works of literature that define a genre, but those pliable librarians who are *also* receptive to trending titles may be better able to recommend readalikes for teens who are interested in advancing beyond the hottest publications to the gems of the genre or even overlooked new authors.

Trends morph quickly, so take this chapter as inspiration. Adapt the ideas to match the fad. Once the tweens and teens have taken to a new celeb, simply adjust the programs provided herein to suit the latest rage.

EEK! Need Justin Bieber trivia questions!—Erin Marsh, Assistant Director, Ransom District Library

PROGRAM

Biebermania

Description

In the '60s, young women fainted over The Beatles. More recently, rising star "the Bieb" has amassed a loyal following of frenzied fangirls. YAACers offer numerous event suggestions for librarians seeking assistance in planning programs that seize upon the zeitgeist of Bieber fever. Once the fervor shifts away from the Bieb, simply tailor the programs that follow to suit the newest face.

The games don't end with mere Justin Bieber trivia. YAACers posted ideas galore. There was even a debate on the list regarding the value of hosting a Bieber ball for the library girls and boys. In defense of such programs, Teen Librarian Karl Siewert argues, "If you have a Justin Bieber ice cream party, and there are 30 kids there, some of them will not have met the others. If you market outside the library with Facebook, Twitter, posters in ice cream shops and music stores, maybe some of them will never have been in the library before. How is that a bad thing?" So, heed Siewert's recommendation. Bieberites unite. Embrace the frenetic ecstasy of Bieber delirium.

Activities

$10 or less

- Create Bieber collages using donated or deselected magazines.
- Spin the singer's tunes in the background.
- Play Justin Bieber trivia (with the warbler's merch for the winners).
    - Teen Services Librarian Kristen Weaver offers, "I just did a Justin Bieber program. We did a lot of trivia games for about an hour and I gave out candy as prizes. I used these quizzes/games."
    - She shares the following links:
        - General Bieber knowledge: http://thepartyanimal-blog.org//Downloads/How_well_do_yo_%20know_Justin_Bieber_Quiz.pdf
        - Song recognition: http://thepartyanimal-blog.org//Downloads/Name_that_Justin_%2Bieber_Song.pdf
        - Word game: http://thepartyanimal-blog.org//Downloads/How_many_words_%20from_Justin_Bieber_%20Game.pdf
    - Weaver adds, "I also had the kids do impressions of him, and the winner got a poster."
- "Give each other manicures with Bieber nail polish: http://tinyurl.com/4ymt8vn," contributes Katie Clark of Illinois' Winfield Public Library.
- "[Try] crafting a giant group fan letter," suggests Children and Teen Librarian Tanvi Rastogi. "The results are sometimes hilarious!"
- Youth Services Coordinator Wendy Allen of Beaufort County Li-

brary asks, "Why not pretend that he's visiting the library?" She provides her Bieber trio of cheery ideas:

- "Have a competition among small groups to see who can make the coolest, slickest posterboard."
- "Make up cheers to get his attention."
- "Test your tweens' and teens' ardor at waving signs and screaming."

Under $30

- Create Bieber collages using teen magazines or promotional literature.
- Munch pizza on Justin Bieber paper dinnerware.
- "Make BIEBERTINIs," proposes Louise Beebe, adult and high school services librarian for Palos Verdes Library District.
  - Crafted by Nate Wiger at Drai's Hollywood, BIEBERTINIs are blush pink smoothies topped with whipped cream. Served in a martini glass, these virgin cocktails blend the flavors of banana, strawberry, pineapple juice, and coconut cream, and come garnished with Blow Pops and Pop Rocks.[1]
- Teen Librarian Rosy Henderson offers, "You could try doing Bieber trivia after they watch the movie, and award the grand prize winner a Bieber doll. I just got my hands on one…he sings!"
- "You could go old school and have them make a mix tape (CD/playlist)," suggests Library Director Erin Joyce of the New Bethlehem Area Free Public Library in Pennsylvania.
- Andrea Graham muses, "What about mini paper Biebs? http://www.4yablog.com/2010/09/celebrity-papercrafts.html." Graham, a youth culture ethnographer and consultant at 4YA: Inspiration for Youth Advocates, adds, "All you need is card stock, a color printer, scissors, and a[n] X-ACTO knife. If you are working with younger, or less mature teens, you can precut the tab incisions."

Splurges

- Karaoke!
- "Make your own music video," offers Joyce.
- "Bieber has a new perfume called Someday. Maybe give a bottle of it away?" One ounce of the fruity Bieber scent costs approximately $35, so Fiction Department Head Janelle C. Martin sug-

---

1. Cruz, Anne Marie, Rennie Dyball, Eileen Finan, Carlos Greer, Jessica Herndon, Marisa Laudadio, Abigail Stern, Michelle Ward, and Blaine Zuckerman. 2011. "the BIEBERTINI!" *People*, February 12, 2007. MasterFILE Premier, EBSCOhost (accessed September 4, 2011).

gests the complementary products, such as the Bieber hair mist ($20) and Someday Touchable Body Lotion ($25) as lower-cost alternatives.

- Pose for pictures with a Bieber standee ($40 at Party City or Amazon.com, featuring the star's trademark vintage coif).
  - "A huge hit," Head of Technical Services Robert Hayes claims. "Worth every penny. The girls loved it. It's a must."

Steps

Before

- Gather purchased, donated, or deselected magazines for a collage project. Procure any other desired program items, such as the Bieber standee, karaoke machine, camera, prizes, etc. Meet with the Friends of the Library to request event funding. Promote the party by tweeting, blogging, and organizing teens to create signage.[2] To secure parental permission, pass out photo release forms. (Sample photo releases are provided in Appendix 1.)

Immediately Prior

- Shop for fresh BIEBERTINI ingredients. Set up crafting tables, karaoke system, blenders, and standee.

After

- Pass out, then review comment forms.
- Clean up the BIEBERTINI activity area.
- Tweet Bieber party pics.
- Show appreciation to the Friends of the Library. Share pictures and comment form opinions.

Cost

- Staff time
- $10-$150 for supplies, depending on prizes, activities selected, and refreshments.

Program Type

Active

Duration

1-3 hours

---

2. Work with library management to determine appropriate marketing opportunities.

Planning Time

1-8 hours

Marketing

Let tweens and teens know that pictures will be tweeted to Bieber. Of the Tewksbury Public Library Bieberites, Hayes posts, "Teens love the possibility of becoming famous. They were so excited when I told them that I was going to tweet the group photos to Justin."

Photograph by Monique Delatte Starkey

Partnerships

"The local press ate this program up," brags Hayes. "One of our print newspapers also came and took photos: http://www.wickedlocal.com/tewksbury/news/x941160199/Tewksbury-teens-have-Bieber-fever#axzz1NQOpNTqk. The photos ended up on the front page!"

Feedback

Hayes used comment forms.

Raves

Hayes' participants uniformly gave the party a positive review in the evaluation form.

Weaver posts, "After all the trivia, we showed the movie. If I judge by how many of them were singing along, I'd say they had a good time."

Web Component

- Hayes' program not only included tweeting the party pics, but was also featured on a local website. "Here are some great photos from our town's online newspaper: http://tewksbury.patch.com/articles/image-gallery-tewksbury-fans-leave-it-to-bieber#photo-6147027," writes Hayes.
- "As scary as this may sound—there is a website, justinbiebergames.org—where fans can post quizzes all about the Bieb," discloses Adult/Teen David Senatore, Estill County Public Library.

Lagniappe

Hayes jokes, "If you use nametags, be prepared for at least half of your teens to write 'Future Mrs. Bieber!'"

Anti-Valentine's Day Party

I am planning an anti-Valentine's Day party," announces Senior Librarian for Teen Services Patricia Foster, Salt Lake County Library System. "I seem to have misplaced my file with most of my ideas!

Description

"Alone on Valentine's Day? Who cares! Party with us in defiance of the love-mongers!" That is the message that Teen Librarian Cindy Simerlink promotes to her teens. She writes, "We ripped apart dollar store teddy bears, defaced romance covers, did romance *Mad Libs*, and smashed candy hearts to decorate cookies. There was also a sour Skittles-eating contest, a breakup letter-writing contest, and spontaneous poster defacement. I put up colored markers and posters that said, 'Celebrities most likely to spend Valentine's Day alone,' 'Most unromantic movie,' and 'Worst Valentine's Day present.'"

Activities

- "I don't know where you can get blank candy hearts, but we take a pill crusher and destroy the ones with the cute sayings!" Mary Rogers shares. "It's a hit every year!"
- "Wrote our favorite heartbreak/anti-love/emo…song lyrics and quotes on a big board," contributes Head of Youth Services Angie Manfredi, Mesa Public Library, Los Alamos, New Mexico.
- "The teens adored ripping apart the plush teddy bears. Some of the boys really went to town with the skewers. One poor bear had nine different skewers!" says Simerlink.

Teens at Huber Heights Branch contribute to an anti-Valentine's Day message. Photograph by Cindy Simerlink

- "Read from *Cringe: Teenage Diaries, Journals, Notes, Letters, Poems, and Abandoned Rock Operas*, and *Love Letters You Were Never Meant to Read*," offers Manfredi.
- "A Match the Doomed Couples game with pictures of Romeo and Juliet, Antony and Cleopatra, Buffy and Angel, Ron and Lavender, Harry and Cho, Sonny and Cher, Adam and Eve, Lady Di and Prince Charles, Marilyn Monroe and Joe DiMaggio, Napoleon and Josephine, Hamlet and Ophelia," proposes Emily Fleischer of Brownsburg Public Library.

Young adults skewer teddy bears in celebration of anti-Valentine's Day. Photograph by Cindy Simerlink

Photograph and display by Monique Delatte Starkey

- "Star-Crossed Lovers," is the title suggestion from Manfredi, who remembers, "The most popular was *definitely* Britney Spears; much merriment was had."

Steps
Before
- Simerlink explains, "I saved e-mails in a folder for a couple years. I presented ideas to my teens at an Advisory Council meeting [and] recorded their preferences. I looked at possibilities and logistics and determined the final plan—95 percent of what they preferred."
- Gather supplies: pill crusher, conversation hearts, sour Skittles, discount teddy bears, skewers (e.g., bamboo), thematic CDs, poster boards and markers, and books, like Bill Shapiro's *Other People's Love Letters: 150 Letters You Were Never Meant to See* or Sarah Brown's *Cringe: Teenage Diaries, Journals, Notes, Letters, Poems, and Abandoned Rock Operas.*

Immediately Prior
- Set up CD player, poster boards, and other supplies.

After
- Pass out pink promotional buttons (description follows).
- Work with teen volunteers and staff to clean up stray teddy bear stuffing.

Cost
- Staff time, 3-9 hours
- Supplies, $0-$50

Program Type
Active

Duration
1-3 hours

Planning Time
2-6 hours

Marketing

"The runaway hit of the party: the pink skull buttons that were party favors.[3] Best library promotion ever! A year later," attests Manfredi, "they still…promote the library with them!"

Partnerships

- "We are getting so much publicity for this event," says Foster. "Yesterday I was on the local TV channel morning news program, and today a large local radio station is coming to interview me about it."
- "Adults are almost more excited about it than the teens," shares Manfredi. "Our entire library staff got into the mood. One part-time staff member even brought 20 black helium balloons as a gift; they were such a hit!" Manfredi reflects, "Everyone remembers how miserable it was to be that person in high school who felt like they were the *only* one left out…I know I sure do."

Raves

"It was well-attended (24 teens), and lots of fun!" enthuses Simerlink. "One of the most-enjoyed programs of the school year. We saw some new kids there that continued to attend. We got several boys."

Web Component

- "Found a Mad Libs website," hints Simerlink, "to select some made by others, and to create my own (http://www.wordlibs.com/index.php)."
- YAACers of Valentine's Day past inspired the 2011 event staged by Simerlink. "I'd had my eye on the posts about anti-Valentine's Day for a couple years, and when I presented it to my teens as a possibility, they were very enthusiastic."

Lagniappe

"Having a movie marathon with my teens of anti-Valentine movies," posts Senior Librarian Christie Gibrich of Bowles Life Center Branch Library, Grand Prairie, Texas. "Anyone have any thoughts on anti-Valentine or Val-

---

3. http://www.etsy.com/listing/18334226/creepy-spooky-skull-button?ref=sr_gallery_5&ga_search_query=skull&ga_search_type=user_shop_ttt_id_21662

Dayton Metro Library teens craft anti-Valentine messages. Photograph by Cindy Simerlink

entine movies that are PG with teen appeal? I am drawing a blank. I'm open to anything at this point—vampires, scary, mushy, whatever."

Stephanie Stokes, owner of LibraryPalooza, replies, "Check out SWANK Movie Licensing USA: http://www.movlic.com/library/index.html. They have a wonderful TOOL for just for libraries! You can also check here : http://www.movlic.com/library/programming.html."

Photos

Art project by Los Angeles young adult Jose Javier. Photograph by Monique Delatte Starkey

Game

Famous Duos

____ Trey Parker	A. Gomez Addams
____ Napoleon Bonaparte	B. Ginny Weasley
____ SpongeBob	C. Luigi
____ Ren	D. Roy
____ Scout	E. Patrick
____ Frida Kahlo	F. Olive Oyl
____ Elizabeth Barrett	G. Brain
__ Barack	H. Ellen
__ Beavis	I. Robert Browning
__ Harold	J. Atticus Finch
__ Pepa	K. Bamm-Bamm
__ Siegfried	L. Matt Stone
__ Starsky	M. Manjula
__ Pinky	N. Edward
__ Thelma	O. Walter Sobchak
___ Mork	P. Kumar
__ Mario	Q. Salt
__ Pebbles	R. Diego Rivera
__ Bella	S. Mindy
__ Apu	T. Josephine
__ Portia	U. Captain
__ Morticia	V. Louise
__ Harry Potter	W. Hutch
__ Tennille	X. Butt-Head
__ Popeye	Y. Michelle Obama
__ The Dude	Z. Stimpy

"I am going to use this for my anti-Valentine's Day program, but it would be easier if you had an answer key for me to use."—Patricia Foster, Whitmore Public Library

Famous Duos: Answer Key

(L) Trey Parker

(T) Napoleon Bonaparte

(E) SpongeBob

(Z) Ren

(J) Scout

(R) Frida Kahlo

(I) Elizabeth Barrett

(Y) Barack

(X) Beavis

(P) Harold

(Q) Pepa

(D) Siegfried

(W) Starsky

(G) Pinky

(V) Thelma

(S) Mork

(C) Mario

(K) Pebbles

(N) Bella

(M) Apu

(H) Portia

(A) Morticia

(B) Harry Potter

(U) Tennille

(F) Popeye

(O) The Dude

A. Gomez Addams

B. Ginny Weasley

C. Luigi

D. Roy

E. Patrick

F. Olive Oyl

G. Brain

H. Ellen

I. Robert Browning

J. Atticus Finch

K. Bamm-Bamm

L. Matt Stone

M. Manjula

N. Edward

O. Walter Sobchak

P. Kumar

Q. Salt

R. Diego Rivera

S. Mindy

T. Josephine

U. Captain

V. Louise

W. Hutch

X. Butt-Head

Y. Michelle Obama

Z. Stimpy

6

Eat Me, Drink Me: Culinary Programs

While library books nourish the expanding minds of growing teens, young people famously crave nutrition for the mortal husk as well. The siren song of food and drink has compelled many a hesitant young adult into the clutches of well-meaning librarians who aim to feed both the spirit and the earthly coil. In this chapter, YA-YAAC contributors serve up tasty programs that teens will devour.

All food programs are a hit.—Librarian Linda Greenbaum, Bethpage Public Library, NY

Excited tweens and teens and a fiery hot stove may not sound tempting, but:

1. The results are delicious,
2. Group gastronomy is a superb learning opportunity, and
3. The teens and tweens who are more comfortable with the saucery will take the mitts.

If you prefer the job of photographer/taster, politely ask (or beg or bribe) your designated library staff baker to take the lead. When selecting an executive chef, remember that cookery programs represent an excellent opportunity to invite library colleagues to pass along cultural traditions.

For example, Youth Services Associate Tinna Mills describes the contributions of a Dutch summer reading program intern who prepared *boterkoek*, a Dutch butter cake.

At one Southern California public library, young adults spent an afternoon baking delicious treats for attendees of an evening lecture by iconic science fiction writer and library devotee Ray Bradbury. Aromatic notes of blueberries filled the meeting room as Library Assistant Todd Bynum led the treat-making. He highly recommends teen cookery programs: "Baking with young adults at the library is always a fun and rewarding endeavor."

Todd Bynum and Celinna Miranda prepare baked goods. Photograph by Monique Delatte Starkey

---

EAT Me
Blueberry-Vanilla Muffins[1]

Vanilla ice cream, melted, 1 pint
Blueberries, fresh or thawed frozen, drained, 1 cup
Unbleached flour, 2 cups
Baking powder, 3 teaspoons
Brown sugar, 3 tablespoons
Salt, 1 teaspoon
Beaten eggs, 2
Butter, melted and cooled, 1/2 cup
Muffin cups

Preheat oven to 350° F.
For easy cleanup, prep muffin tin with butter cooking spray.
Add muffin cups to tin.
Mix dry ingredients.
Using a different bowl, mix ice cream, eggs, and butter.
Pour all mixed ingredients in one bowl, blend to moisten dry ingredients.
Fold in blueberries.
Pour blueberry batter into muffin tins.
Bake 35 minutes or until a toothpick poked into muffin pulls out without muffin bits.

---

1.   Recipe by Monique Delatte Starkey.

YA Librarian Kathleen Gruver shares, "We just had a really fun Cupcake Boss program today, and I'm feeling ambitious!" She suggests a baked edible in the Halloween vein, noting, "I am also going to try my hand at making these." Gruver then posts a link to instructions for creating delicious, yet visually revolting, brain cupcakes: http://familyfun.go.com/recipes/brain-cupcakes-688207/. Pair the braincakes with a toasty autumn-themed beverage.

DRINK Me
Hot Pineapple Yum Drink[2]

Pineapple juice, 24 oz.
Sweet and sour, 4 oz.
Cranberry juice, 1/2 cup
Brown sugar, 1/3 cup
Cinnamon, 1/2 teaspoon
Nutmeg, 1/8 teaspoon
Cloves, a pinch
Cinnamon sticks to garnish, 3

Mix the ingredients in a saucepan and bring to a boil.
Lower heat and simmer uncovered for 15 minutes, then strain.
Garnish with cinnamon sticks.

PROGRAM

Taco Time!

In Indiana, Alexandrian Public Library's Dana Cohlmeyer posts, "My TAB kids came up with a catchy program title (Taste of Tacos). Has anyone done anything like this? I'm at a bit of a loss! Help...

Need an easy meal? Try tacos. Taco-making programs are a perfect fit for the young adult crowd, balancing safe food preparation with do-it-yourself fun, freedom, and a dash of messy silliness. From cilantro to avocado, the right mix of ingredients may include sifting in the talents of those library staff members who are taco dinner aficionados. The staffers will get a kick out of sharing their expertise with the oft-maligned and misunderstood teens. Any chance to meld teen activities and library staff should be seized.

---

2.   Recipe by Monique Delatte Starkey.

Young adults benefit from the knowledge shared, while library workers are reminded of the joyful energy and excitement about learning that teens bring to the table.

Steps

Before

- Purchase frozen ingredients, paper goods, and plasticware. Coordinate with local grocers or eateries to request donations or a partnership. Cynthia Stanczak of Albion District Library coordinated with a nearby grocery to procure preheated ingredients. Consider serving a vegetarian meat substitute like soy or veggie crumbles by Morningstar Farms or Boca. Stanczak recommends providing a selection of crunchy taco shells, flour tortillas, and corn tortillas. "Consider nacho chips with salsa or guacamole, or warm mole sauce (usually available in a small jar in the Mexican section of most mega-marts) to put on the corn tortillas."
- Promote the event.

Immediately Prior

Purchase and chop fresh ingredients such as tomatoes, peppers, cheese, and lettuce. Set up tables with toppings.

During

Teen librarians suggest:
- "Fried ice cream is always a crowd pleaser: http://www.bettycrocker.com/recipes/cinnamon-fried-ice-cream/bd0cc397-09bb-4eeb-9bac-6d1f525e9561," testifies Andrea Graham.
- Reference/Youth Services Coordinator Marianne Raley says, "We are doing something similar for our summer library program. Instead of tacos, we are doing a fruit salsa and baked tortillas." Raley's young adults will make Guatemalan worry dolls and develop book talks on titles with Spanish or Latin characters or authors. She adds, "I'm also waiting to hear back from a mariachi band from a local restaurant."
- Teen and Technology Services Librarian Danielle Fortin proposes, "You could always make salsa and/or pico de gallo from scratch with them. Or make tissue paper flowers." The Chesley Memorial Library librarian suggests visiting the Family Fun website for instructions to create pepper-shaped piñatas: http://familyfun.go.com/crafts/mini-pinatas-668588/.
- Cohlmeyer announces that her teens will try Mexican hat dancing "for my amusement."

After

- Work with teen volunteers to wipe down the tables and generally clean the area.
- Market YA services by sharing information about successful events such as Taco Time or Taste of Tacos via email, social networking sites, library marquees, or corkboard.

Cost

Inexpensive

- Staff time:
  - This is an event for which well-trained teen volunteers may serve as replacements for staff members.
- Program costs:
  - Plan to purchase ingredients, plastic cutlery, paper plates and cups, and craft supplies (as needed).

Program Type

- Active
- Great for tweens and teens

Duration

1-3 hours

Planning Time

2-10 hours

Partnerships

- Suggests Stanczak, "You might also contact…restaurants to see if they want to partner for the event." She advises that the collaboration is worthwhile "even if it's just for a gift certificate door prize in return for promotion at the event."
- Piqua Public Library's Maria Vega recommends, "I would also talk to a local Mexican restaurant or a local Chipotle. We have had a ton of things donated from them at my library. Our local restaurant also special orders things…like sodas with real sugar. We just get a ton of free chips and salsa."

Tips

Library friends or staff members may be interested in participating, perhaps by sharing cultural traditions or preparing local dishes.

Lagniappe

Wet your whistle. Adult and Teen Services Stanczak invites colleagues to consider serving non-alcoholic sangria, fruit nectars, and soda that is *hecho en Mexico*: "Things your kids might not have tried."

Passion Fruit Virgin Margarita[3]

Fresh passionfruit, 2/3 lb. (or 1-1/2 cups passion fruit juice)
Limeade, 24 oz.
Orange juice, 2/3 cup
Sugar, 1/5 cup
1 lime, juiced
Raspberries for garnish

Halve the passionfruit and scoop the seeds and pulp into the blender.
Blend the pulp briefly, leaving seeds sizable.
Push the passionfruit through a fine sieve back into the blender, discard the remaining solids.
Blend ½ cup puree with all remaining ingredients until smooth.
Pour into three glasses, refrigerate until ready to drink.

San Gabriel Valley teens enjoy pan dulce, a Mexican sweet bread donated by staff members interested in sharing traditional Mexican treats. Photograph by Monique Delatte Starkey

---

3. Recipe by Monique Delatte Starkey.

PROGRAM

Ohm & Yum: Yoga & Smoothies

Description

Teen Librarian Adriana Melgoza brings healthy fun to the Southern California teens of Alhambra Library with an annual yoga and smoothie-making program.

Steps

Before

- Preregister participants (Alhambra Library limits the event to 25 teens).
- Provide participants with liability forms to be signed by parents.

Immediately Prior

- Purchase ingredients (list follows).
- Melgoza suggests, "Lay down tarp or newspaper in case of spills."

Program

- 25 minutes of yoga class, led by a librarian, yoga teacher, library assistant, or teen(s)
  - Supplies: Yoga mats ($12-$15 via amazon.com or participant-supplied), yoga DVD (Says Melgoza, "We used *Yoga for Young Bodies* produced by Acacia in 2004. It has different seg-

Teens at Alhambra Library follow a yoga instruction video. Photograph by Adriana Melgoza

ments that are 30 minutes long, easy to follow, and not too strenuous." Melgoza has also used *Hemalayaa's Yoga for Young Bodies*.)

- 35 minutes of blending smoothies
  - Supplies: Table, cups, napkins, straws, ingredients (such as fruit, yogurt, oatmeal, ice cream, sherbet, vanilla extract, orange juice, milk), blenders (may be borrowed from staff or participants)

After

- Wash blenders.
- Clean up food.
- Wipe down tables.
- Spray mats with Lysol.

Cost

- Staff time
- $25-$50 in supplies, not counting yoga mat purchases

Program Type

Active

Duration

1 hour

Planning Time

Varies, 1-3 hours

Marketing

According to Melgoza, "There are months and days that could lend themselves to coinciding with the themes of health and fitness, such as National Yoga Day in January, National Nutrition Month in March, World Health Day in April, or Family Health and Fitness Day in September."

YA Involvement

Of her Teen Advisory Board members, Melgoza says, "They helped by operating blenders during the smoothie portion of the program, so they earned volunteer credit as well as the opportunity to partake in the smoothies."

Partnerships

- Local grocers, such as Henry's Markets, Whole Foods, or Trader Joe's, are often willing to provide ingredients or a store chef to teach the smoothie portion of the class.
- Nearby yoga studios may be interested in offering a free yoga instruction session.

Feedback

Melgoza explains, "We have done the program for three years, and every year, our Teen Advisory Board members comment that they really enjoy doing something healthy (but low-key), and getting to make their own smoothies."

Raves

"This year teens even asked to do an additional 30 minutes of yoga because they were enjoying it so much!" says Melgoza.

Modifications

Jennifer Trusty, children's librarian at Brazoria County Library System, suggests:

- Provide water.
- Ask teens to wear loose-fitting clothing.
- Request that participants bring beach towels or mats.

Web Component

Teen events at Alhambra Library are promoted via Facebook,[4] the library website,[5] and MySpace.[6]

Lagniappe

See Appendix 1 for liability release form.

PDFs and Photos

"We used frozen fruit," says Melgoza. "Strawberries, mixed berries, mangoes, as well as fresh bananas. We also had milk, soy milk, plain yogurt, ice cream, artificial sweetener, sugar, and honey available."

4.　http://www.facebook.com/alhambrateens
5.　http://www.alhambralibrary.org/teens/TAB.html
6.　https://myspace.com/alhambrateens

Photographs by Adriana Melgoza

Yoga & Smoothies

Ohm & Yum!

Teens, join us for some relaxing yoga (If you have a mat, please bring it. If not, we will have some available). After the yoga session, we'll blend up some yummy and healthy smoothies.

**REGISTER AT
THE TEEN DESK**
(Waiver Required 17 & under)

Thursday, April 28th 2011

3pm

Reese Hall

Questions? Teen Desk: (626) 300-1549

Alhambra
Civic Center
Library

101 S. First St.
Alhambra, CA 91801

Phone: (626) 300-1549
E-mail: alhambrateens@gmail.com
 alhambralibrary.org
myspace.com/alhambrateens
facebook.com/alhambrateens

Flyer by Adriana
Melgoza

No-Bake Quickies

Has anyone ever done a no-cook or no-bake program with their teens?—Lindsay James, First Colony Library Youth Services Paraprofessional

Hurricane Party

Weighing in from a hurricane-prone area of the U.S.—Palm Bay, Florida—Youth Services Librarian Jennifer Hopwood of Franklin T. DeGroodt Memorial Library responds, "I used to do [a no-cook program] as part of our Summer Hurricane Party (this is the first year I haven't done one). I start with canned chicken and go from there." Her tips include, "Check out camping cookbooks, Boy and Girl Scout manuals, and emergency preparedness websites/blogs. Children's cookbooks usually have some great, easy no-cook recipes." She plugs preparedness, saying, "I always centered mine around the idea that there is no electricity (including fridge)." Hopwood suggests Googling "baggie ice cream and eggless cookie dough. Both are no-cooking."

She lists:

> S'mores pudding—Shelf stable chocolate pudding cups, crushed graham crackers, and mini marshmallows.
>
> Taco salad—Lettuce, canned tomatoes (drained), crushed nacho Doritos, and taco sauce/French dressing.
>
> Southwest chicken salad—Canned chicken, ranch dressing, canned black beans, and canned corn.
>
> Guacamole—Seasoning mix, onion, avocados, lime, and chips.
>
> Dirt cups—Chocolate pudding, crushed Oreos, and gummy worms.
>
> Candy sushi—Rice Krispies treats, Swedish fish, fruit roll-ups OR Twinkies, and licorice.
>
> Pita pizza—Pita bread, pizza sauce, and Parmesan cheese.

Agua Fresca Fun

David Gallin-Parisi tells YAACers, "We've done some agua fresca programs at my branch in San Antonio, Texas. The no-cook sessions are super fun. I used my own cutting boards since our branch doesn't have any yet. Also, I brought a sharp cutting knife of my own." He advises, "The recipes are really easy, but do involve a decent amount of chopping, mixing, straining, and stirring. Plus, lots of hand-washing and fruit-washing." The Teen Services Librarian at San Antonio Public Library pitches his preferred resource, *Paletas,* as "a book that has great recipes for agua fresca," particularly favoring the cucumber lime agau fresca.

"I did a no-cook program with a Mexican theme, we made watermelon agua fresca with blenders [and served] salsa and guacamole," contributes Jamie Micka, a librarian for the *Muskegon Area District Library* Norton Shores Branch. Rather than bring supplies from home, Micka "had everyone bring their own knives, cutting boards, and storage containers." She assures risk-averse colleagues, "It worked out great—no one was missing fingers at the end!"

Salsa Soirée

Fruit and veggie lovers can also find their fix with Library Media Specialist Katherine (Kat) Kan at St. John Catholic School. Kan offers, "If you have a farmer's market handy, you could buy these fruits (peaches, melons, oranges, pineapple, mango) along with cucumbers, fresh cilantro, limes, red onions, and jalapenos without spending too much money. The fruits can go a long way—one $5 watermelon would provide enough fruit for maybe 20 batches of salsa, for example." Kan tells YAACers of "a mixed berry salsa that can go on top of ice cream—strawberries, blackberries, kiwifruit, sugar, lime juice, and chopped basil." The deliciousness of these healthy treats doesn't come too easily, though; Kan's caveat is that there is "lots of chopping involved." However, she reminds YAACers that the salsa requires no cooking and is healthy. Kan's resource recommendation is *Parenting* magazine's recipes for five fresh salsas using fruits, available via http://www.parenting.com/gallery/salsa-recipes.

Regardless of the direction you choose to go, display salsa cookbooks and don't forget the chips!

Chopped No-Cook Challenge

Katie St. Laurent of *Fayetteville Free Library* posts, "Just this week we did a chopped no-cook cooking challenge, where we gave the kids a bowl full of mystery ingredients that they were required to use in their creations, plus a pantry table of optional items. We did three rounds and had three judges. The kids had 20 minutes each round to make something out of the items in their bowls, then present three finished samples to the judges. They were judged on originality, taste and presentation. They had a blast!" St. Laurent recalls that in "the first round they received pitas, cream cheese, celery, and bacon; round two was raisins, marshmallow fluff, and a fruit cup; and round three they got pickles, a tomato, a basil leaf, [and] a taco shell." Teens could also incorporate additional ingredients. "Optional items included vanilla pudding, ham, lettuce, dressings and other veggies," says

St. Laurent. "You could make it more or less challenging by the foods you give them"; teen participants "were stumped because they didn't recognize the basil!" St. Laurent challenges colleagues, "If your teens would rather compete than do an activity or a lesson, this might be a fun option!"

Reading is Sweet!

Not all of the no-cook noshing festivities feature concoctions that are as healthy for everyday consumption as the refreshments served up at agua fresca and salsa events. Pueblo City-County Library District Teen Librarian Maria Kramer concedes, "All my no-cook cooking programs have been extremely unhealthy!"

Kramer is looking forward to an upcoming candy construction event. To prepare, New Mexico librarian is consulting *Candy Construction* by Sharon Bowers. She explains, "I found plans for a large, ambitious castle made out of cookies. I thought it would be cool for a group of teens to make the castle and decorate it collaboratively." This sugar plum librarian listens to volunteers' opinions and shares a creative teen twist on the idea: "One of my teen volunteers suggested hosting group competitions between different libraries."

Oakland City-Columbia Township Public Library Director Julie Elmore entreats teens to participate in a Reading is Sweet program by offering events such as "decorate your own cupcake day, cookie day, candy plants, clown sundaes, and candy sushi." The Indiana-based director reveals, "I bought the library a cotton candy machine." How did her teens react? They were "totally intrigued." Her syrupy style is proving popular; as she says of her teens, "They lined up in droves to volunteer for clown sundaes!" In a succulent finale, summer reading program participants doused Elmore in cocoa syrup, ice cream, and toppings, then topped her off with whipped cream at the Reading Wrap-up Party.

Let Them Make Cake Pops

"Just did cake pops for the first time and it was a huge success. If anyone is thinking of doing it in the future, here are a few tips," offers Adult and Young Adult Services Librarian Katie Clark. "I got 200 munchkins from Dunkin Donuts as the base and it worked out perfectly. I went there a week ahead of time and asked if I could have that many plain cake donut holes made without glaze." Clark retrieved the baked goods in the morning, and stored the doughnut holes in the refrigerator "until the afternoon program to help keep them firm for dipping." She adds, "I also bought some Oreos and marshmallows as additional things to dip in whatever chocolate was leftover. I used half milk chocolate and half vanilla flavored candy melts from Michaels, melted them in the microwave, and kept them warm in crock pots during the program." She warns, "Make sure you keep stirring!" Next, Clark's teens "ladled out chocolate into individual bowls and dipped from those." Clark also acquired lollipop sticks, sprinkles, and colored sugar at arts and crafts supply store Michaels, and had nuts and chocolate chips for toppings. (When registering for the event, young adults were required disclose food allergies.) Clark gets down to brass tacks: "The program went very well but it was not cheap—about $200 for 15 participants, so be aware of that. Tons of pictures are at http://winfieldya.wordpress.com/2012/07/11/delicious-cake-pops/."

Jumping in from the tri-state area, good-natured Public Library Director Julie Elmore blurts out, "Wow. That seems really expensive. No way could I justify spending $200 on any program." She explains that her cake pop program was "generic. We didn't allot that many pops to a person. We used blocks of almond bark from the grocery store. Then we bought a cake from the bakery day-old rack, scraped the icing, and wallah." Elmore quips, "The person doing the program liked the older cake because it was a little dryer. We liked it because it was 40% off."

"I also would never be able to get $200 for a program like that," commiserates Nicole Cubero, a Hillsborough County library technical assistant. The Florida library services worker thanked Clark for "insight on the process" and remarked that she will search for "ways to cut down on the expenses."

Reference and Teen Librarian Lori-Ellen Smith of Stafford Library responds, "To save money, instead of using donut holes, make cake mixes. You make the cake in a rectangle pan [and] when it is cool, put the cake into a bowl and squish it into crumbs. Add about 2/3 of a can of frosting and mix it all together. Form it into balls and freeze the balls for about 1/2 hour before you stick the sticks into them. Then you can coat them with the chocolate and decorate."

Maria Kramer comments, "I traded money for time and baked six cakes of different flavors to make into cake pops. We used different colors of meltable candy bark that I got from Hobby Lobby, plus sprinkles." She describes the event as "fun, but very, very messy."

"You also don't have to use the melting chocolates unless you feel like you want the 'candy' coating," recommends Senior Librarian Christie Gibrich. "I can't stand the taste of them, so when I make them...I use chocolate chips, either the [normal kind] or white chocolate," says the Texas epicurean.

Rhode Island gourmand and Warwick Public Library Teen Librarian *Liz* Gotauco observes that cake may be replaced by "scraps from sugar cookie dough" as in the blog post: http://prudentbaby.com/2011/03/entertaining-food/cookie-crumb-truffle-pops-2/. She suggests, "Flatten it and bake, then crumble it. Not technically 'cake' but it sure sounds yummy."

Gotauco wonders, "How [have] those of you who have done this made it a good group project? I am thinking of doing it with my TAC for our first meeting. I thought it would be fun, since you assemble bits of it, then those have to set before the next step. (I'm thinking we'll talk TAC stuff while things set)."

Kramer replies, "I've done cake pops with my TAB and it worked great! I brought in big bowls of the cake batter mixed with frosting so that teens could mold their own. That was fun, but requires a powerful freezer to set the pops enough to decorate later. I've heard people recommend the pops be pre-made and pre-frozen, in which case teens would just decorate them."

Whether formed of cake crumbles, cookie scraps, or doughnut holes, these delectably tasty treats are a guaranteed crowd-pleaser!

Easy English Muffin Pizzas and Pages

From no-cook s'mores to Pizza and Pages book clubs, library workers nationwide have become experts at throwing together quick cookery programs for appreciative teens. Laura Mesjak of Cortland Community Library in Illinois posts, "I bought an inexpensive toaster oven. Last month we made English muffin pizzas with great success." Mesjak's favorable outcome shows how no-fuss teen events can be just as enjoyable as programs that require extensive planning.

Fudge It: Brainstorming

Katie Clark of Winfield Public Library fudges the no-cook rules, prodding, "If you're able to use just a microwave or small appliances like a crock pot, there's a ton you can do. Try http://www.kidactivities.net/category/Snacks-No-Bake-Recipes.aspx." Clark rattles off a few stove-free program possibilities, including "different dips like taco dip that just need mixing and layering of ingredients, the classic kick-the-can ice cream-making, haystack cookies, Oreo balls..." She gleefully adds, "Caramel apples, fondue, and fruit pops."

Whether the fare is healthful or...less so, vittles-filled programs are a fun way to share cultural foods, normalize healthy eating, or just reach out to teens, nourishing both the body and the natural human desire for rewarding social interactions in a safe space.

7

Over Twenty Quickies for Free (or Practically Free)

Just christened as young adult services librarian by my library manager, but there's no program budget. What should I do?

This is the classic conundrum that bedevils many newly inducted YA librarians: commencing teen services sans cash, connections, institutional knowledge, or support. Though overwhelmed, the librarian consumes programming literature; consults teens, staffers, and email discussion lists; contacts nearby school librarians, counselors, and teachers; and slings caution to the gale, embracing the challenge and succeeding in making teens feel welcome in their library.

Fledgling teen librarians aren't the only young adult services professionals who could use novel programming ideas that stretch emaciated budgets—so take heed, seasoned and newbie librarians. Savor the fruit of the YA-YAAC list. YAACers[1] have been finding and sharing hundreds of cheap programming suggestions for more than a dozen years. Enjoy these 20 fresh programs that encourage innovation in your library!

---

1. Major contributors to the inexpensive programming list discussion include, but are not limited to Young Adult Services and Reference Librarian Katie Spofford, Wadleigh Memorial Library, Milford, NH; and Adult/Teen Programmer David Senatore, Estill County Public Library, Lexington, KY.

Clubbin'

1. Book Clubs: Kick off your tenure as teen librarian by taking advantage of interlibrary loan to amass copies of a hot new title for a YA book club.
2. Fan Clubs: Offer space for teen fan club meetings. YAs can share fan fiction, chat about favorite characters, and dish about the leaked book draft or sultry star pegged for the leading role in a movie adaptation.
3. Anime Clubs: Start an anime club! Hand out pencils and paper so teens have the option of drawing while watching the flick. Contact anime film companies to request free preview copies.

Citing the YA-YAAC list, Las Vegas librarian Sarah Oakie blogs, "I had no clue where to start. Luckily, the collective brain over at YA-YAAC had lots of suggestions." She extols her "favorite resource so far," which is "Operation Anime, a DVD request service from the Funimation studio." Of the one DVD that is mailed monthly, Oakes attests, "They always send you the first disc of season 1, which has 6-7 episodes to hook in your viewers. The series selection is pretty impressive (considering you're getting titles from only one studio), and runs across a good many genres." As for the downside, she explains, "The series tend to be newly released (and probably unfamiliar to most of your teens), so one can imagine why Funimation might want feedback on these hot off the presses series."[2]

TAG!

4. Hosting a teen advisory group/board meeting provides an opportunity for young adults to form new friendships, meet their teen librarian, and vote on or propose programming. Tween and Teen Librarian Chrissie Morrison, of East Greenbush Community Library, writes, "My TAG meetings usually have food at the end as a 'thank you' and an incentive to show up and participate, but food is not necessary!"

Wet & Wild

5. Aqua Competitions: For the price of a jumbo bag of balloons, a bucket, and a sponge, teens can be entertained for hours. Inexpensive and easy, this idea begins with allowing young adults to fill water balloons at a spigot, and ends with any number of

---

2. Oakie, Sarah. "Anime club." Posted April 21, 2011. http://advocateen. wordpress.com/ (accessed September 2, 2011).

games, e.g., hot potato toss, balloon squat relay race, and sponge relay races. Says YAACer Katie Spofford of Wadleigh Memorial Library in Milford, New Hampshire, "All you need is a patch of lawn and a hose!"

6. Beach Ball Bowling: Set up water bottles like bowling pins, and toss some strikes! Allow teens to determine whether to roll according to United States Bowling Congress regulations or develop new rules of play.

Theater

7. *MST3K* Party: In the tradition of *Mystery Science Theater 3000*, screen a public domain film, silence the audio, and encourage teens to improvise dialogue. If a few bucks are available for refreshments, set the mood by serving popcorn washed down with soft drinks.

8. Improv or Prop Comedy Show: Teens are tossed random objects and, in Chicago's Second City-style, must use the props to elicit laughter from the audience. In one version of this game, two or more teens are given a few objects to work into a silly infomercial performance.

Literati

9. Writing Workshop: Seek local poets and authors to donate their time to lead workshops for teens. Break the ice by reading your in-workshop piece first, if teens are reluctant to swap.

10. Book Swap: Reduce, reuse, recycle with a hip library book swap. Katrina McCurley of Concord Public Library writes, "We did host a successful paperback book swap club. The kids provided their own paperback books to swap, and we provided a space and snacks." Various libraries have implemented and adapted this program. Tying up summer programming, teens of the Fargo Public Library participated in a teen art show and book swap.[3] At Dekalb Public Library, teens receive volunteer hours for swapping, and if the book trades are uneven, participants give one another credit towards the next swap.[4] In Washington, Camas Public Library's book swaps have become so popular that they've drawn more than 100 participants.[5]

---

3. http://fargolibrary.areavoices.com/2011/07/28/library-hosts-teen-art-show-and-book-swap-august-2-and-4/

4. http://dcplive.dekalblibrary.org/2009/02/09/book-swapping-with-the-teens/

5. "Camas Library lets readers swap children, teen books." March 26, 2011. *The Columbian* (Vancouver, WA). NewsBank.

11. Poetry Slam/Beatnik Coffee House Open Mike Night: Encourage young adults to explore the beauty of the spoken word by bringing their poetry to present for an audience of their peers.

12. Book Crush Fête: Teens gather to gab about interpretations of favorite novels, beloved characters, and cherished tales. To play book crush bingo, make bingo cards featuring the names of the debonair dudes and lovely ladies of literature, and replace bingo daubers with chocolate confections or conversation hearts. Sellers Library Young Adult Librarian Gretchen Ipock describes her Upper Darby, PA book crush soirée: "It was so much fun to hear everyone's crushes, opinions, and reactions. We played book crush bingo (really an excuse to eat chocolate), made beaded bookmarks with a crush's name on them, wrote personal ads for our crushes, and decorated heart balloons. Of course, there was lots of food and lots of discussion of book boys!" She adds, "I'd say it was a success!"[6]

13. Book Speed Dating: Teens skim a novel for five minutes, then complete a brief survey about the likelihood that they would select that novel for pleasure reading.

14. Hunger Games: Union County Public Library's Grace Dow challenges libraries to attempt the Scholastic *Hunger Games* virtual training competitions, Trial by Fire and Tribute Trials, available via http://www.scholastic.com/thehungergames/games/index.htm. The North Carolina children's and teen services librarian explains, "If computer access is possible, tributes can try competing in one of Scholastic's two online training games." Dow's teens earned points on a scorecard for completing each challenge.

Fun with Science

15. Lunar Sample Disk: For an out-of-this-world teen event, borrow a lunar sample disk from the Johnson Space Center. NASA will even cover the cost of shipping to *and* from your library! A lead time of six weeks is required. To request the disk, email Jsc-curation-education-disks@mail.nasa.gov or shoot a snail mail to Mary K. Luckey, NASA/JSC, Mail Code KT, Houston, TX 77058.

---

6. http://sellerslibraryteens.blogspot.com/2009/02/book-crush.html

Lunar sample disk. Photograph by Monique Delatte Starkey

Financial Education

16. Playing the Market, Virtually: Lori-Ellen Smith recommends http://stockmarketgame.org/. Depending on sponsorship levels in the region, the price ranges; however, it is free in many areas. Librarians may also be interested in trying similar free sites such as WeSeed (http://www.weseed.com/education). Smith instructs, "You register teams [and] each team gets a pretend $100,000 account to invest over a period of a few months. They should meet regularly, usually weekly, to look at the account and decide as a group what stock to buy or sell. You could provide snacks and books or magazines about investing, and the stock market game site provides activity ideas for what you do with them."

   Anythink Commerce City Youth Services Guide Colleen Watson contributes, "Another idea is the Hollywood Stock Exchange: http://www.hsx.com." Watson explains, "It gives them the same information, but instead of companies, you buy, sell, trade [stock in] movie/TV stars." The Rangeview Library District worker says, "It's a fun time. It helps that most kids are so tuned into popular culture." Online videos (such as http://www.metacafe.com/watch/4180112/teach_money_to_kids_using_the_hsx_com/) show how the tool is used in teaching.

Arts & Crafts

17. Zentangle: If you can doodle, you can zentangle. Discovering doodling-as-art is fun for both budding artists and novices. Use interlibrary loan to finagle zentangle books. Zentangle involves working a sketch on paper until the image morphs, or tangles,

into a recognizable shape or intersecting series of shapes. Artists will use a pen or pencil line to define specific areas or shapes.

Encouraging young people to discover their inner doodler might also help inattentive teens to focus in the classroom, according to research published in *Harvard Business Review*: "Unlike many dual task situations, doodling while working can be beneficial. Future research could test whether doodling aids cognitive performance by reducing daydreaming."[7]

18. Cubeecraft: For libraries with cardstock on hand, Burlington County Library System YA Librarian Kathleen Gruver recommends visiting http://www.cubeecraft.com to gather great paper-crafting ideas. She describes the parchment-bending crafts as habit-forming, saying, "Cubeecrafts are quite addictive—I have a Tardis, a Totoro, and a Gir (from Invader Zim) sitting on my desk." Download the foldable cube templates from the site, then print and copy for teens. This craft requires cutting, so Gruver's laidback teens use scissors and craft knives. Concerned about risk or liability? Pre-cut, instructs Youth Services Clerk Dedria Tillett of Upland Public Library.

Photograph and drawing by
Monique Delatte Starkey

---

7. Hallowell, Edward M. "Overloaded Circuits: Why Smart People Underperform." *Harvard Business Review* 83, no. 1 (January 2005): 54-62. *Business Source Elite.* (accessed September 16, 2012.

Photograph and Cubeecraft gone wrong (a lunar rover vehicle). Photograph by Monique Delatte Starkey

19. I Spy: "A fun photo program is I Spy," promises *Voice of Youth Advocates* Editor-in-Chief RoseMary Honnold. "This can be done as an easy, independent program. Take a photo of some unique feature of your library or community, zoom in on it, and crop it to print. Post it and ask teens to identify it, and where it is in the library. Examples are pieces of art, or sculpture, or architectural features, advertising logos, and signs." To culminate, Honnold suggests, "The next day, post the whole photo with the answer, and put up a new one to guess."

20. Goth Sock Puppets: Oh my gock! Spartanburg County Public Libraries Teen Services Assistant Heather Price asks, "Can someone direct me to a good Gock (Goth sock)-making tutorial?"

Teen Services Librarian Patricia Foster replies, "As the proud creator of the original Gocks program idea, here is the article from *VOYA*,[8] which gives you all the information and lists supplies." She shares the link https://sites.google.com/site/libraryprogramideas/ tweens-teens/gocks, then continues, "If you are interested in seeing some photos of Gocks, I could send those, too. Glad to see Gocks are still going. It is a fun activity!"

21. Butt Pillows: Describing her fashion program, Circulation/ Technical Services Assistant Sandra Miller shares, "The kids brought in an old pair of jeans…cut the legs off them, sewed the leg holes together and proceeded to glue or sew on decorations." She suggests, "Staff would probably be willing to donate bits of lace and other types of materials (plastic jewels, patches, etc.), then give the kids some fabric markers, or regular markers borrowed from the children's area, and let them decorate their pillows. They can be stuffed with strips of old sheets, old socks and pantyhose, old towels, whatever. Then sew up the waist and you have a really cute pillow!"

22. T-Shirt Pillow Program: "Kids brought their own T-shirt (with parental permission), and cut it into two equal squares. We then cut strips and tied them together like a fleece pillow,"

Photograph by
Monique Delatte
Starkey

8. "GOCKS! GOTH SOCK PUPPETS FOR TEENS." 2006. *Voice of Youth Advocates* 29, no. 4: 303. *Library, Information Science & Technology Abstracts*, EBSCOhost (accessed September 24, 2011).

recollects Stacey Strickland, assistant director and youth services coordinator for Stevens County Library.

"Another good pillow stuffer—used dryer sheets. I collect mine for stuffing pillows. Ask staff members to save them for you. Post a sign asking patrons to give you their used dryer sheets," hints Kat Kan, school librarian and collection development librarian for Brodart's books division in Panama City, Florida.

Warns Strickland, "A word of caution: once you start holding craft projects, the kids will *beg* for them. That may be a way to convince management to increase funding!"

Still nervous about planning programming? Consider the advice of Adult/Teen Programmer David Senatore of Estill County Public Library: "Play to your strengths." Share passions, talents, hobbies…your excitement will be contagious, and library teens will demand more! And don't forget to post questions or program ideas to the YA-YAAC list. A colleague will likely reply with tips to help smooth the rough edges of any event idea. Too shy to post? Shamus-like, become a fly on the wall of the YA-YAAC email discussion list by signing up and reading the steady stream of emails, whether in digest form or one-by-one. Worried that the email discussion list will usurp an already beleaguered inbox? Consider the advice of Librarylion's Lounge blogger, *Charleston County Public Library* Business Reference Librarian and fiction writer Amanda Holling: "**Subscribe to YA-YAAC.** You'll get so many good ideas." Holling writes that following a two-week intermission from the email discussion list, it "only took about 20 minutes to go through."[9] Alternatively, set an email filter to automatically archive YA-YAAC updates in a dedicated file and go through them at your leisure. (Sign up to receive YA-YAAC at http://lists.ala.org/sympa/arc/ya-yaac or http://lists.ala.org/sympa/lists/divisions/yalsa.)

Replies and questions are posted to the listserv by young adult services librarians, children's librarians, media specialists, school librarians, after-school program workers, information science graduate students and faculty, and other library workers who offer teen programming. Often greeting YAACers with "Hello, great brain," listserv users recognize what a tremendous resource the archive represents. Spread across the nation, continent, and even the world, the listserv is a virtual information mother lode just waiting to be tapped. Colleagues, though scattered across time zones, seamlessly congregate online to disseminate knowledge, offer encouragement, and act as a sounding board for ideas. It's free. It's available 24/7. The YA-YAAC listserv truly is a great brain with an incredibly democratic purpose.

---

9. http://librarylionslounge.blogspot.com/2006/11/musts-for-ya-librarians_15.html

8 Practical Advice

Planning

Preparing for teen events can be a time-consuming endeavor. Planning might include researching program ideas; securing funding; booking performers, space, and/or help; marketing the event through school visits, posters, word-of-mouth promotion, flyers, newsletters, and/or email or text message announcements; shopping for materials or requesting donated materials; preparing craft samples; developing and dispersing feedback forms; gathering library resources to share; and much more. Many of the programs described in this book include information regarding the preparation time required. Teen services professionals who lack significant preparation time should consult Chapter 1 for passive programming ideas.

Execution

The easy part. The planning is done, or it isn't, and now the chips fall where they may. The teens show up, or they don't. The Zapp's Gator-Tators, Pocky sticks, baklava, or apple slices *will* be devoured…either by two dozen teens or three supportive library pages. YA librarians and library staffers can prepare, but attendance can't be controlled. If the program proves a bust due to lack of warm bodies, accept that young adults (1) sometimes participate in extracurricular activities at the dictate of their parents, (2) often have unreliable transportation, and (3) must prioritize school work before library activities. **Don't let a flop stop your teen services.** That is an overriding message of the email discussion list. "Burnt Out," an August 2011 post regarding a lack of teen interest in the programming efforts of a youth services librarian/interim library manager, garnered more than fifty responses from sympathetic YAACers. YA-YAAC advice for increasing program attendance includes:

1. Survey teens for program requests.
2. Increase outreach (by visiting middle/high schools).
3. Coordinate with teachers to plan lunchtime book clubs on campus, or give extra credit to students attending educational library programs, such as book clubs, author visits, or SAT/ACT prep courses.
4. Provide after-hours and anime-related programs.
5. Offer month-long contests that teens can participate in remotely, such as digital scavenger hunts.
6. Incorporate local motifs, such as Comic Con-themed events for Southern California, or live band competitions during music festivals like New Orleans' Jazz Fest or Austin's SXSW (South by Southwest) music, film, and interactive festival.
7. Have a sign-up sheet and require a small deposit (e.g., $5) that will be returned upon attendance.
8. Award volunteer hours for attendance.
9. Grant double volunteer hours to participants who bring a friend who has never before attended a YA event at the library.

From New Hampshire's Keene Public Library, Gail Zachariah offers a sage reply to the "Burnt Out" post: "Programs come after collections and connections."

Still not attracting the crowd size you desire? Remember that teens' time is limited. Need reliable attendance? Start a book club for retirees.[1]

Feedback

I've been given the task of developing a program evaluation strategy for my library and I'm struggling with where to begin.—Amy Dawley, Prince George Public Library, British Columbia, Canada

Frequent posters to the email discussion list offer varying tips for event appraisal. Some list contributors suggest talking with the participants at a teen advisory board meeting or casually in the library. Other YAACers pass out comment forms immediately following every event. YA-YAAC list posters also employ online surveys, such as SurveyMonkey and other virtual survey tools.

---

1. Not that there's anything wrong with that.

Sample Program Feedback Form[2]

Name: _____

Age: _____

Grade: _____

Email: _____

	Agree	Partially agree	Disagree	Recommendations
The performer presented the content in a compelling way.				
The program was held at a good time.				
The program was held on a good day of the week.				
This was fun!				
I learned something new.				
This program increased my interest in library resources, like books and databases.				
How did you find out about this program?				
What other programs would you be interested in attending?				
Comments				

THANKS!

---

2. Sample feedback form by Monique Delatte Starkey

Marketing Library Services for Teens

How have you been able to promote the program to get participants?—Paige Garrison, Bartow County Public Library

Contributors to the YA-YAAC list approach library services marketing from a variety of perspectives. Easily replicated advertising and outreach ideas sprinkle in from all over the United States. Referring to her teen book club, Belvedere-Tiburon Library Teen Librarian Rebecca Jung shares that "for marketing, we just do flyers, email, [and] word-of-mouth." As libraries confront staffing shortages in a tough economy, simple marketing plans such as Jung's become increasingly viable.

Old-fashioned word-of-mouth promotion is popular among YAACers. Elizabeth Seeskin of Crete Public Library in Illinois remarks, "I have always found that talking to teens is more effective than flyers. They tend to block out visual noise around them and assume that things that involve leadership and planning aren't meant for them. Whenever I've started a program, I make an effort to talk to every teen I see in the library and invite them individually."

Jennifer Senger of Berrien Springs Community Library agrees, "I still make flyers, but I do try to catch teens in the library, too. I have had teens come to programs because I talked to them personally. Believe it or not, they had never noticed one of my brightly colored signs." Adds Senger, "It helps build a relationship."

If library staff coverage permits, visit nearby middle and high schools to market library programs to young adults. Senger attended her local high school's orientation night to promote her TAG. YAACers can also work to coordinate with local teachers, do classroom booktalks, or provide lunchtime book clubs on campus.

Warwick Public Library Teen Librarian Elizabeth Gotauco visits classrooms to promote their library card sign-up month. She explains, "We have a form that we send home to schools and the kids can sign up and receive their cards through the classroom." Gotauco adds that when visiting local schools at the beginning of the academic year she will "take that time to also promote our Teenspace and any September/October programs we'll have coming up."

YA-YAAC list contributors also considered the pros and cons of text message promotion. Youth Services Librarian Allison Boyer argues that "a lot of [teen library users] have only a certain number of minutes, and they don't want to sacrifice them." Boyer's teens tend to prefer the *Loutit District Library* online teen program calendar. Head Librarian Kristen Corby remarks that the choice of whether or not to use text messages to promote library programs "really does depend on the nature of your patron base."

Visit these online resources for more ideas regarding how to promote library services for young adults:

- http://yalibraryuk.wordpress.com/2010/07/22/where-to-do-out-reach-for-teen-library-services/
- http://www2.scholastic.com/browse/article.jsp?id=3747845
- Acknowledging that "young adults are entitled to the same quality of library services offered for other age groups in the population," this document features a great section regarding advertising programs to young adults (section 5): http://archive.ifla.org/VII/s10/pubs/Profrep107.pdf

Promoting YA services to Friends of the Library (FoL), library management, staff, and the community:

- http://yalibraryuk.wordpress.com/2011/02/10/against-cuts-teen-library-literac/

Information and inspiration for librarians promoting YA programming:

- The initial paragraph of this resource is especially relevant: http://broadbandsummit.mel.org/toolkitresources/AmericanLibraryAssociation-InternetConnectivityinU.S.PublicLibraries.pdf

YALSA intermittently releases prewritten letters to the editor used by librarians to promote YA services in concert with parents, teens, or library friends. (See Appendix 1 for an example.)

Securing & Maintaining Partnerships

YAACers coordinate with authors, local businesses, teachers, national entities, various government departments, and, of course, Friends of the Library groups to bring value to teens' library experience. Partnerships can be complex, including letters of agreement and financial support, or simple, e.g., one city department lending an item to another. Chippewa River District Library System's Tinna Mills borrowed a green screen from her local parks and rec department.

Outreach Support

Every YA librarian should be prepared to defend the young adult services budget. Teen services may be the first department that admins are itching to slice and dice. Outreach to teens is often a newer endeavor, while entrenched services are less likely to be viewed as expendable. Bring attention to your accomplishments and the value of your outreach efforts (especially circulation stats).

Building Partnerships with Funders

1. Court the Friends of the Library.
   Perhaps the most viable fundraising opportunity is to approach

the FoL. The care and feeding of library friends is key to earning ongoing support for resources and events. Attend Friends' meetings (invite library teens to attend); have young adults create and sign thank you cards for the Friends; disclose to the Friends precisely how their monies benefit the library teens.

2. Reach out to local businesses.

   Librarians may send annual letters to nearby brick and mortar sales establishments; call; or knock on doors, meeting with managers and owners at opening time on a slow business day. Youth Services Librarian Ami Segna has been successful in partnering with businesses to promote library summer reading programs with primo prizes. She notes, "One year we had a local bank donate a laptop."

3. Seek support from organizations.

   Community-focused organizations may be able to offer funding or other forms of support. For example, through coordination with the Chamber of Commerce, West Covina Library was able to bring in local professionals to speak with teens about entrepreneurship and budget management. La Puente Library received funding for gaming equipment from non-profit organization Children's Council of Los Angeles County Service Planning Area Three.

4. Approach large businesses to request support.

   Corporations and other large businesses can be a resource for ex-

Remind teens to fill out comment forms and sign thank you cards to funders before jetting! Photograph by Monique Delatte Starkey

pertise, product, time, or money. Partnering with businesses can be an inexpensive way to provide high-quality educational experiences for teens.

Lowe's assisted Tippecanoe County Public Library with a Huckleberry Finn-inspired project when the library participated in a community reading event, One Great Read. The title being discussed was *The Complete Short Stories of Mark Twain*. Interested in developing a complementary program, Young Adult Librarian Melissa Delaney contacted the local Lowe's, who was willing to donate all of the materials and time into building the raft (a scale model), and even sent a store employee to the library to explain how it was built, what materials were used, and more.

Janelle C. Martin, Fiction Department Head of the Lapeer District Library, Marguerite deAngeli Branch, shares, "If you write to the Duck corporation, they might be willing to send you several rolls of free duct tape to use for a program."

- Contact information for Duck® Products:
  - ShurTech Brands, Attention: Consumer Relations, 32150 Just Imagine Drive, Avon, Ohio 44011
  - Call center: 1.800.321.1733 (9:00 a.m.–4:00 p.m. EST)
  - http://www.duckbrand.com/Info/Contact.aspx
  - Corporate offices: 150 Fairview Road, Mooresville, NC 28117 (704.799.0779)
- *Editor's note:* Duck® Products parent ShurTech annually sponsors the scholarship competition "Stuck at Prom." Ask the library friends or a local hardware store to donate a few rolls! More details at http://duckbrand.com/Promotions/stuck-at-prom.aspx

5. Charity begins at home.
Share the good news about library programs at the family reunion, during pigskin bowl parties, amid award season fêtes, and between swishes at the dentist's office. Donations will spring forth. Friends, family, and professional service providers enjoy hearing positive news about teen volunteerism, learning, and outreach in the community. Your ophthalmologist might not be able to give, but may connect you with contacts interested in community giving. Be open to unexpected opportunities!

6. Collaborate with natural allies.
Raise funds by working with book vendors and authors. West Covina Library coordinated with Barnes & Noble to raise money for teen programs. Young Adult Board members distributed a flyer asking that patrons shop at the bookstore on a particular morning. Shoppers who presented the flyer when making a purchase on

a specific date, during a set range of hours, were guaranteed that a portion of sales would be dedicated to the library's Friends group.

Fantasy and science fiction author Ray Bradbury was a tremendous supporter of libraries. When he agreed to visit West Covina Library, young adults prepared for the occasion by creating foam board posters, each featuring one of the prolific author's book covers. Over the course of his life, Bradbury wrote more than two dozen story collections and novels—so many, in fact, that the newly constructed signs encircled the entire library community room, overlapping slightly. Bradbury mused, "I never knew how much I'd written until I saw this" (gesturing towards the posters). He provided contact information for a representative at HarperCollins, so that the library Friends could purchase his books below cost, then sell the titles to raise funds. Bradbury even arranged in advance for the library to send back any unsold copies. Bradbury gave his lecture, then patiently autographed over 100 books and posed for photographs with library patrons. Young adults who had no experience with Bradbury's work prior to the lecture became obsessed with devouring the prolific author's oeuvre for months following the event.

Free lectures are a great way to raise money for the library through the sale of friends' books. The Friends of the Library may reap financial benefit from a spike in foot traffic in the book sale area following a speaker visit. Authors who provided no-cost lectures for La Puente and West Covina Libraries include Lisa Yee, an Asian-American author for the *American Girl* and other series, and writer of the YA title *Absolutely Maybe*; Melissa de la Cruz, the Filipina-American author of the *Au Pair* and *Blue Bloods* series; Brandon Noonan, author of YA title *Plenty Porter*; and Linzi Glass, author of young adult title *The Year the Gypsies Came*.

Local writers aren't the only intriguing community members who may be willing to donate time to lecture and raise cash for the library. In regions with a thriving film industry, such as New Orleans, Austin, New York, and Los Angeles, librarians may wish to invite locals with a silver screen background to speak with young people. La Puente-born, Hispanic-American comedian and voice actor for films such as *Happy Feet*, Jeff Garcia inspired the kids of La Puente Library with his story of success. Garcia provided a humorous and motivating lecture in which he briefly roasted the librarian, teasing, "We're going to teach Ms. Monique how to say 'La Puente' right!" West Covina Library young adults enjoyed a lecture by library user and Grammy-nominated composer William Peele, an African-American artist and entrepreneur whose fashion designs can be seen in films such as David Lynch's *Wild at Heart*.

North Branch Summit County Library Branch Manager Janet Good shares that she's "had good luck finding interesting local people to come speak" at no charge. Popular speakers include a rescue dog handler, the county coroner, a uranium mine-finding geologist, a detective who demonstrated crime scene investigation, a children's book illustrator, a Red Cross trainer discussing pet first aid, and a former Ice Capades skater.

7. Hunt for grant offers.

   Stay current via e-subscriptions. Librarians can be in the know about newly opened grant opportunities by subscribing to free, frequently updated, library grant blogs and e-newsletters. Sign up for the RSS feed at http://librarygrants.blogspot.com, developed and maintained by the authors of *Winning Grants: A How-To-Do-It Manual for Librarians with Multimedia Tutorials and Grant Development Tools*, Stephanie Gerding and Pam MacKellar. This tremendously helpful site is regularly updated with new opportunities. Another invaluable resource for grant-hounding is the no-cost e-newsletter, *Quinlan Grants for Libraries e-News Alerts*. Subscribe via http://west.thomson.com/signup/newsletters/209.aspx.

8. Develop a boilerplate.

   A boilerplate is a prepared statement that can be popped into any funding request letter or grant app with minimal tweaking. It should be a statement that describes the library as worthy of financial support. Write the statement in a straightforward, persuasive manner. The boilerplate assists funders in determining the applicant's point of view. It shouldn't be self-pitying, but rather outline the situation and how the library is overcoming challenges. It is a paragraph that clearly presents the library as the outside world should view it. Determining what is unique about the community will help in creating a boilerplate. U.S. Census figures affirm that what librarians experience every workday is quantifiable, whether it is proving that the city's young adult population is greater than the national average, or that the number of unemployed is especially high, or that there are an atypically large number of single parent homes. The census may provide the information required to develop a cohesive, convincing argument that the library's teen services are worthy of grant monies. Completing a boilerplate means that a significant portion of any grant is already finished. (A boilerplate sample is provided in Appendix 1.)

Working with Young Adults

Volunteers

Queries regarding teen volunteerism pop up frequently on the email discussion list. Coinciding with the start of the fall semester, a North Carolina librarian asked what job-training opportunities YAACers provide for teen volunteers. Within minutes of the post, replies sprang forth from all across America! California, Missouri, Indiana, Ohio, and Massachusetts were among those represented in the flood of swift responses to this question from Fayetteville.

Leadership, technology, instructional, and planning skills are developed by the teens actively participating in learning opportunities at libraries from coast-to-coast. Teacher-like bulletin board duties are assigned to Glendale Public Library teens in Arizona. San Antonio teens prep crafts, shelve books, and adhere to a dress code. In Amesbury, Massachusetts, teens run clubs to earn volunteer hours. At Allen County Public Library, thirty Fort Wayne teens are selected as summer hires and trained to act as reading coaches for kids through the grant-funded program Team Read. In the Northeast, young adults lead book clubs for Swampscott Public Library. Creative teens in Monmouth Junction, New Jersey, write and perform plays in the library. Podcasting is popular among the Midwestern young people at Kirkwood Public Library in Missouri. The tweens and teens of Richfield Branch Library bring their anti-cyberbullying message to local schools and Akron Children's Hospital. From southwest Quebec, a youth resources librarian posts that volunteerism is not permitted in her library due to union concerns regarding job protection, so YAs participate in a teen council, computer classes, and library gaming activities. In the greater New York City area, at New Milford Public Library, Valerie Fisher's young adults stage programs for children, including Renaissance and science fair(e)s.[3]

---

3. Major contributors to the discussion of preparing teens for the workplace include, but are not limited to: Teen Services Librarian II Merideth Jenson-Benjamin, Glendale Public Library, Glendale, Arizona; Library Assistant Sylvia Pachecano, City of San Antonio, Texas; YA Librarian Margie Walker, Amesbury Public Library, Massachusetts; Young Adult Services Manager Mari Hardacre, Allen County Public Library, Fort Wayne, Indiana; Young Adult Librarian Sandy Moltz, Swampscott Public Library, Massachusetts; Young Adult Librarian Saleena Davidson, South Brunswick Public Library, Monmouth Junction, New Jersey; Teen Coordinator Chris Durr, Kirkwood Public Library, Missouri; Teen Librarian, Adult Librarian, Branch Manager Jen Stencel, Richfield Branch Library, Akron, Ohio; Youth Resources Section Head Caroline Cyr La Rose, Dollard-des-Ormeaux Public Library, Quebec.

Led by the Los Angeles artist Roxana *Ocaña* Torres, teens assist with library science fair activities. Photograph by Monique Delatte Starkey

Staff

Consultant and learning designer Marc Prensky is the author of several titles that address the information-seeking habits of young people, such as *Teaching Digital Natives: Partnering for Real Learning* and *Don't Bother Me Mom—I'm Learning!* In the piece *Digital Natives: The Changing Face of Education and Workforce,* a consideration of the role of libraries and education in the lives of the Internet Generation, Prensky stresses the importance of providing services and outreach to young people. Prensky warns that if libraries lose this generation, then library services will become irrelevant, no longer garnering tax monies or public respect.[4] Paco Underhill, noted author and environmental psychologist, echoed that sentiment when addressing Los Angeles County Library librarians following an assessment of patron use of county libraries in 2007.

Convincing staff of the importance of catering to young adults is a challenge that is commonly confronted by teen librarians. Creating buy-in among the library team for increased teen presence in the library is imperative to developing a welcoming environment for young adults. How should a new YA librarian convince entrenched or overworked staffers that expanding services to high-energy tweens and angsty teens is a worthy endeavor? One solution is to combat resistance by offering staff the opportunity to become personally invested in the success of teen outreach. To encourage staff investment in young adult services, use the strengths of the library team to improve the visual appeal of the YA stacks, or to lay

---

4.   Keynote speech. Urban Libraries Council Partners for Success: Changing Face of Cities Conference, May 4, 2007, Cleveland, Ohio.

out the teen area. Staff members gain a stake in teen services by suggesting program ideas and assisting with implementation. Team members could help plan cultural programming, provide direction, suggest vendors, or teach young people how to prepare traditional dishes. Stage events that utilize employee input to remind staffers (the backbone of the library) of how rewarding it is to share cultural customs, and bond with young people (the future of the library).

YAACers Quick Tips to Encourage Staff Buy-In

- "Leftovers go to the staff lounge," posts Alamogordo Public Library Youth Services Librarian Ami Segna, "[as] minor compensation for the inevitable extra noise."
- Sharon Savage of New Castle Public Library writes, "How well do your teens know each other or does your staff know the teens?" Savage suggests playing the guessing game Who's Behind the Mask? "You could come up with leading identity questions or your teens could write a Who Am I? type script."

Advisory Groups
Generating Teen Interest

A YAACer inquires as to how other librarians approach starting a teen advisory board from a *tabula rasa* in a post entitled, "Building a teen program from scratch?" Posters often recommend that newbies start YA services by offering teens the opportunity to meet and discuss what they want from the library. If the FoL is willing to provide $30 for pizza, drinks, and paperware, a pizza party and meeting is a reliable afterschool draw. Ask a nearby middle or high school to announce the event over the intercom system one week in advance, and on the morning of the meeting. (Remember to order a vegetarian pie for the conscientious crowd!)

No dough? No problemo! Work with teachers to incentivize participation via extra credit. Librarian Linda Greenbaum posts to the list, "We have a very good relationship with the school media specialists and do joint programs, reserves, etc. We plan to have a table at open school nights and have an open house for teachers so they can learn what resources we have for students." Greenbaum divides young adult duties with another librarian, together dedicating a total of 8-15 hours per week to teen services. No time for outreach to the schools? Advertise the programs as a superb opportunity to earn volunteer hours.

If time allows, create an itinerary for each young adult board gathering. An itinerary can serve as an impressive deliverable to be presented to library friends and management. Itineraries also assist in keeping young adults focused on issues and goals. Bring in guest speakers to address the young adult board—instant programs, instant audience! Consider inviting a library user or friend who is familiar with *Robert's Rules of Order* to discuss meeting protocol with the teens—perhaps a speaker who can address college prep or dinner party etiquette is on the library staff roster. For special occasions or holidays, rope in a relevant presenter, such as a parent or local dignitary who can share cultural information. Perhaps a local poet or an English professor can teach haiku in April for National Poetry Month.

Teen Services Librarian II Merideth Jenson-Benjamin's Teen Library Council selects a project to complete. Allowing the group to select initiatives helps develop project buy-in among participants. Often, a leader will emerge to keep the peer pack on task and to assign jobs to project members. At the Glendale Public Library, teens usually choose to stage an event. Teens are encouraged to pitch ideas, then these suggestions "evolve in interesting ways based on budget and policy," explains Jenson-Benjamin. "At the first meeting, we make a rough calendar of when all these programs could happen. So, the group that's working on a zombie program, that's a good fit for October." To celebrate Teen Tech Week™, tech activities are scheduled for March. Climate is also a consideration in calendaring teen programs, says the Arizona librarian. "Planning a sports day? Let's save that for February." Her teens use a form to associate event ideas with realizable steps.

1

Templates and Samples

The following samples and templates provide a starting point. Tailor these examples to fit your library.

Sample Grant Boilerplate

The La Puente Library, a County of Los Angeles Public Library, serves the community of La Puente, California. The name of our city translates to "the bridge." *The La Puente Library is very much a bridge between an exciting, growing, majority Hispanic community of recent immigrants and the learning resources that today's libraries can offer new citizens.* According to the U.S. Census 2005–2009 *American Community Survey*, this community is 83% Latino, and nearly three-quarters of the citizens of La Puente speak a language other than English at home. The U.S. Census Bureau reports higher-than-average poverty rates and low education levels here that are a challenge to community supports. We are seeking your support in our mission to encourage La Puente teens to visit the library for fun *and* to discover the learning resources offered, which include a Homework Help Center and an active teen volunteer program that brings in 30-40 teen volunteers each month.

Sample boilerplate by Monique Delatte Starkey

Letter to the Editor Template

This letter to the editor adapted from the Teen Tech Week website, www.ala.org/teentechweek.

[insert date]

[insert name]

[insert address]

[insert name]
Opinions Editor, *[insert name of periodical]*
[insert address]

To the Editor,

As a parent of a teenager, all the negative stories I hear on the news and read in the paper about teens are troubling. I know that most teens do not engage in illegal behavior like the ones portrayed in the news, but I worry about my teen being exposed to some of the dangers that are so prevalent in today's society. I would just like to state that there is at least one place in our community where teens can go and are encouraged to engage in positive activities, and that's the local school and public libraries. My teen uses the [INSERT YOUR LIBRARY NAME HERE] for more than homework and school projects. They have a wide selection of reading materials including magazines, graphic novels, and books, as well as provide interesting, age-appropriate, and free programs like [INSERT PROGRAMS AT YOUR LIBRARY; e.g., Princeton Review College Prep, Salsa for Teens, and Young Adult Journaling]. I also like that the library offers a wide variety of technology and has staff that are knowledgeable. With all the new technologies, it's difficult to keep up as a parent, so it's good to know that there are adults who are on top of all the new trends and can assist my child in a positive way.

I'd like to encourage other parents to make a trip to the library with their teenager to check it out. There are more great resources and events than most parents would think, and there are trained professionals who can help you get your questions answered. Plus, it is a place where teens can engage in positive activities.

—Parent of a library teen

Letter to a Partner Template

Adapted from YALSA's Advocacy Toolkit at www.ala.org/yalsa/handouts. Use this sample letter with partners to gather support.

Dear [CONTACT NAME]:

What a pleasure and satisfaction it's been to work with you on our Poetry Slam for teens! It has been a wonderful project thanks to you and many others. The program is unique in providing a free activity that promotes literacy and is fun for kids. Attendance has grown consistently over the last three years, and there has been great feedback from kids and teachers.

Unfortunately, the Poetry Slam is in jeopardy because of proposed funding cuts to our library. If the cuts are enacted, the library will no longer be able to stay open on Friday evenings, and teens will lose the space and assistance provided by library staff. There will be other cuts as well. The city council will discuss the library's budget at its next meeting on [DATE]. I hope you and your organization will want to attend or contact the mayor and your city council representative to let them know how important this program is to teens and our community.

Thank you again for your past support. We look forward to working with you in the future.

Sincerely,

Librarian Name

Sample Release Form

GOSHEN PUBLIC LIBRARY
Read.Play.Move
Teen Summer Reading Experience 2011

INFORMATION FOR PARENTS/LEGAL GUARDIANS

We are pleased that you have given your child permission to participate in our programs for the Teen Summer Reading Experience 2011 (TSRE) at the Goshen Public Library. These programs are intended for those in grades 6–12, and we ask that children younger than this not participate in these programs.

Please read and sign this permission/waiver/release form. You may drop off the form at the Library's main desk anytime before the first program you wish to attend. <u>No one may participate without a signed permission/waiver/release form.</u>

TIMES for pickup and drop-off will range for each program. Please check with Circulation staff if you have any questions about the times for each program. All events will be **SUPERVISED** by two or more Library employees. The **dress codes** will vary with each program and are subject to change due to weather; please check with the Library staff before the program. **Everyone will be expected to have their permission/waiver/release form with them if they did not turn it in earlier.**

*If an emergency situation arises and you need to contact a staff member immediately, the contact phone number for all events is 533-9531 unless otherwise notified.

PHOTOGRAPHS

I also give **consent** to Goshen Public Library staff to photograph, film, or videotape my child, and to use the photos, digital reproductions, or film with or without my child's name for the library's website or in other official library publications. I acknowledge the library's right to crop or treat the photograph at its own discretion.

Goshen Public Library is not responsible for unauthorized duplication or use by third parties including on the Internet. This release is valid until revoked and applies to multiple times and uses. Goshen Public Library has no liability for any use made before the Library Director receives my written revocation.

PLEASE PRINT

NAME OF PARTICIPANT_____
BIRTH DATE_____

PARTICIPANT'S ADDRESS_____
HOME PHONE_____

NAME OF PARENT/GUARDIAN

_____

PHONE # OF PARENT/GUARDIAN IN CASE OF EMERGEN-CY_____

IS THERE ANYTHING WE NEED TO KNOW ABOUT YOUR CHILD/TEEN? (food allergies, health issues, medications, etc.) *If you need more room, please use the back of this form.*

_____

WAIVER AND RELEASE FROM LIABILITY (PLEASE SIGN AND INITAL WHERE INDICATED)

(I) (WE) Sign _____ do hereby COVENANT NOT TO SUE, AND RELEASE and forever DISCHARGE the Goshen Public Library and its agents, directors, officers, and employees, from all actions, charges, demands, damages or claims for relief on account of any and all injury which may exist or which may hereafter arise from participation in <u>any</u> GPL summer program in which my child/teenager participates. (I) (WE) do further agree to protect the said Goshen Public Library and its agents, directors, officers, and employees, from any damages or liabilities of any kind whatsoever incurred by way of claim, demand, or judgment and agree to reimburse the Goshen Public Library for any loss, damage or cost incurred. (I) (WE) am/are 18 years of age or older, and that (I) (WE) executed the above foregoing WAIVER AND RELEASE

FROM LIABILITY and that such are true and correct to the best of (my) (our) knowledge and belief, this _____ day of _____ 2011.

(I) (WE) HAVE READ THIS DOCUMENT AND UNDERSTAND THAT IT IS A RELEASE OF ALL CLAIMS. **(Initials)**_____

SIGNATURE OF PARENT/GUARDIAN IF PARTICIPANT IS UNDER 18 YEARS OF AGE:

X_____

DATE:_____

Form courtesy of Ann-Margaret Rice, Head of Adult and YA Services, Goshen Public Library, IN

Teen Volunteer Application Form Template 1

[Insert name of library]

[Insert year] Teen Volunteer Application

Name: _____

Age: _____ (Must be 18 and under)

Volunteer street address: _____

City and zip code: _____

School attending: _____

Dates: _____

Phone number(s): _____

Email: _____

Total volunteer hours to be earned: _____

Availability: _____

How did you hear about this volunteer opportunity?

_____

I agree that the information submitted in this application is true.

Volunteer signature: _____

Date: _____

Parent or guardian signature: _____

Date: _____

[Insert library contact name]

[Insert name of library]

[Insert library street address, city, state, and zip code]

[Insert library telephone number]

Teen Volunteer Application Form Template 2

How to Volunteer at [insert library name]

1. Please complete this volunteer form to the best of your ability. We expect that you are able to complete the form on your own, and return the form with a parent or guardian signature.
2. When you begin working as a volunteer, we expect that you will both sign in and personally check in with a library staff member.
3. Please start by renewing or getting a new library card at [insert location, e.g., front desk]. Renewing or getting a new library card earns you two volunteer hours!
4. Please sign out for the day twenty minutes prior to library closing. Please inform your parent or guardian that they will need to pick you up twenty minutes prior to library closing.
5. If you have a computer at home or school, you may start earning hours by visiting [insert library social networking site], and watching the videos about how to volunteer at the library. Watching the how-to videos earns you two volunteer hours!
6. If you would prefer to volunteer from home, you may submit book reviews (videos or written) for the library [insert library social networking site]. Hours awarded will be determined by the teen outreach coordinator, and are dependent upon the quality of the submission(s).

[Insert library name] YOUNG ADULT V VOLUNTEER APPLICATION

VOLUNTEER NAME: _____

ADDRESS: _____

DATE OF BIRTH: _____

EMAIL ADDRESS: _____

HOME PHONE: _____

CELL PHONE: _____

JOB HISTORY: _____

_____

EDUCATION, SKILLS, OTHER LANGUAGES SPOKEN:

_____ _____

_____

ALL STATEMENTS MADE IN CONNECTION WITH MY
VOLUNTEER APPLICATION ARE TRUE TO THE BEST OF MY
KNOWLEDGE.

VOLUNTEER SIGNATURE: _____

DATE: _____

PARENT OR GUARDIAN SIGNATURE: _____

DATE: _____

PARENT OR GUARDIAN NAME: _____

PARENT OR GUARDIAN PHONE: _____

EMERGENCY CONTACT NAME: _____

EMERGENCY CONTACT PHONE: _____

[Insert library contact name and contact information]
[Insert library name, phone number, address, and hours]

Teen Volunteer Application Form Template 3

[Insert library name] Teen Volunteer Application
[Insert library name, phone number, street address, city, state,
and zip code]
[Insert library mission statement]

Volunteer expectations:
1. Volunteers must provide their own transportation.
2. Volunteers are expected to be considerate of other library users.
3. Volunteers should expect to be assigned projects during designated volunteerism hours only.

Designated volunteer hours include:
[Insert day of week] [Insert start time – end time]
[Insert day of week] [Insert start time – end time]
[Insert day of week] [Insert start time – end time]
[Insert day of week] [Insert start time – end time]

What will I be asked to do as a volunteer?
[Insert library name] offers a variety of volunteer opportunities. You may be asked to assist in the homework center, shelve books, help with the preparation of story time crafts, and, eventually, train new volunteers!

1. Name: _____

2. Grade: _____

3. Address: _____

4. Date of birth: _____

5. Phone number: (____)_____

6. Email address: _____

7. Work and volunteer history: _____

_____ _____

8. Hobbies and skills: _____

_____

9. Languages spoken: _____

_____

10. Education: _____

11. Availability (dates/times): _____

12. Emergency contact information: _____

_____

13. Contact information for at least one personal

reference: _____

_____

Statements made in this volunteer application are true.

Volunteer signature: _____

Date: __/__/__

Parent name: _____

Parent or guardian signature: _____

Date: __/__/__

Parent or guardian contact information:

_____

Teen Volunteer Application Form Template 4

Date: __/__/__

First initial of last name: ____

[insert name of library] [insert year] Young Adult Volunteer Application

Welcome! We appreciate your interest in working as a volunteer for [Insert library name]. Volunteering is a great way to enhance your college application, meet new friends, gain work experience, and lend a helping hand to your community.

- We ask that volunteers earn hours by helping at programs.
- Please see the monthly flyer for information about the upcoming events.
- Volunteers may arrive as soon as 45 minutes before an event. Volunteers will be asked to: help set up *prior*, participate *during*, and assist in cleaning up *after* the event. If gaming is offered after an event, you may also earn volunteer hours by assisting with and participating in gaming events.
- Story time is considered an event.
- When you arrive, please introduce yourself to a library employee, and inform that employee of your intent to volunteer.
- Once the event begins—enjoy the show! Your mature presence in the audience helps to set a calm tone and positive example for young participants.
- There may be occasions when we ask you to assist with other tasks (based on your performance at events).

We look forward to working with you at [insert library name]!

Name: _____

Date of birth: __/__/__ (Must be 12-18 years of age.)

Street address: _____

City, zip code: _____ , _____

School: _____

Grade: _____

Home number(s): _____

Cell: _____

Email: _____

Number of volunteer hours desired: _____

Availability: _____

How did you discover this volunteer opportunity?_____ _____

_____

Is there any additional information that you would like to share? _____

_____

_____

Parent or guardian name: _____

Relationship to applicant: _____

Cell: _____

Home and work phone number(s): _____

Street address: _____

City, zip code: _____ , _____

Emergency contact name: _____

Relationship to applicant: _____

Cell: _____

Home and work phone number(s): _____

Street address: _____

City, zip code: _____ , _____

Doctor name and phone number: _____

I hereby agree that the information submitted in this application is true.

Volunteer signature: _____

Date: __/__/__

Parent name: _____

Parent or guardian signature: _____

Date: __/__/__

Parent or guardian contact information:

_____

Photography Release

I grant [insert library name] permission to photograph and film me/my child for reproduction via [insert library name] Web pages, in [insert library name] publications, and in [insert library name] displays. These images may be edited. These images may be used to promote [insert library name], without compensation. These images may be used in a newspaper, report, or other public document. These images may be used in presentations to promote [insert library name]. These images may be used with or without identification by name of me/my child. I will not hold [Insert library name] responsible for unauthorized re-use of these images.

Volunteer name: _____

Volunteer signature: _____

Date: __/__/__

Parent name: _____

Parent or guardian signature: _____

Date: __/__/__

Parent or guardian contact information:

_____

[insert library contact name and contact information]
[insert name of library, library street address, city, state, and zip code]
[insert library telephone number]
[insert library hours]

Teen Volunteer Time Sheet

Volunteer name: _____

DATE	TIME IN	LIBRARY EMPLOYEE SIGNATURE	TIME OUT	LIBRARY EMPLOYEE SIGNATURE	TOTAL

Grand total: _____

Volunteer signature: _____

Supervisor signature: _____

2

YALSA's Competencies for Librarians Serving Youth: Young Adults Deserve the Best

Updated January 2010

Introduction

The Young Adult Library Services Association (YALSA), a division of the American Library Association (ALA) that supports library services to teens, developed these competencies for librarians who serve young adults. Individuals who demonstrate the knowledge and skills laid out in this document will be able to provide quality library service for and with teenagers. Institutions seeking to improve overall service capacity and increase public value to their community are encouraged to adopt these competencies.

YALSA first developed these competencies in 1981, which were revised in 1998, 2003, and 2010. The competencies can be used as a tool to evaluate and improve service, a foundation for library school curriculum, a framework for staff training, and a set of guiding principles for use when speaking out for the importance of services to teens in libraries.

Audiences for the competencies include:

- Library educators
- School and library administrators
- Graduate students
- Young adult specialists

- School librarians
- Library training coordinators
- Public library generalists
- Human resources directors
- Non-library youth advocates and service providers

Area I. Leadership and Professionalism.

The librarian will be able to:

1. Develop and demonstrate leadership skills in identifying the unique needs of young adults and advocating for service excellence, including equitable funding and staffing levels relative to those provided for adults and children.
2. Develop and demonstrate a commitment to professionalism and ethical behavior.
3. Plan for personal and professional growth and career development.
4. Encourage young adults to become lifelong library users by helping them to discover what libraries offer, how to use library resources, and how libraries can assist them in actualizing their overall growth and development.
5. Develop and supervise formal youth participation, such as teen advisory groups, recruitment of teen volunteers, and opportunities for employment.
6. Model commitment to building assets in youth in order to develop healthy, successful young adults.
7. Implement mentoring methods to attract, develop, and train staff working with young adults.

Area II. Knowledge of Client Group.

The librarian will be able to:

1. Become familiar with the developmental needs of young adults in order to provide the most appropriate resources and services.
2. Keep up-to-date with popular culture and technological advances that interest young adults.
3. Demonstrate an understanding of, and a respect for, diverse cultural, religious, and ethnic values.
4. Identify and meet the needs of patrons with special needs.

Area III. Communication, Marketing, and Outreach.

The librarian will be able to:

1. Form appropriate professional relationships with young adults, providing them with the assets, inputs, and resiliency factors that they need to develop into caring, competent adults.
2. Develop relationships and partnerships with young adults, administrators, and other youth-serving professionals in the community by establishing regular communication and by taking advantage of opportunities to meet in person.
3. Be an advocate for young adults and effectively promote the role of the library in serving young adults, demonstrating that the provision of services to this group can help young adults build assets, achieve success, and, in turn, create a stronger community.
4. Design, implement, and evaluate a strategic marketing plan for promoting young adult services in the library, schools, youth-serving agencies, and the community at large.
5. Demonstrate the capacity to articulate relationships between young adult services and the parent institution's core goals and mission.
6. Establish an environment in the library wherein all staff serve young adults with courtesy and respect, and all staff are encouraged to promote programs and services for young adults.
7. Identify young adult interests and groups underserved or not yet served by the library, including at-risk teens, those with disabilities, non-English speakers, etc., as well as those with special or niche interests.
8. Promote young adult library services directly to young adults through school visits, library tours, etc., and through engaging their parents, educators, and other youth-serving community partners.

Area IV. Administration.

The librarian will be able to:

1. Develop a strategic plan for library service with young adults based on their unique needs.
2. Design and conduct a community analysis and needs assessment.
3. Apply research findings towards the development and improvement of young adult library services.
4. Design activities to involve young adults in planning and decision-making.

5. Develop, justify, administer, and evaluate a budget for young adult services.
6. Develop physical facilities dedicated to the achievement of young adult service goals.
7. Develop written policies that mandate the rights of young adults to equitable library service.
8. Design, implement, and evaluate an ongoing program of professional development for all staff, to encourage and inspire continual excellence in service to young adults.
9. Identify and defend resources (staff, materials, facilities, funding) that will improve library service to young adults.
10. Document young adult programs and activities so as to contribute to institutional and professional memory.
11. Develop and manage services that utilize the skills, talents, and resources of young adults in the school or community.

Area V. Knowledge of Materials.

The librarian will be able to:
1. Meet the informational and recreational needs of young adults through the development of an appropriate collection for all types of readers and non-readers.
2. Develop a collection development policy that supports and reflect the needs and interests of young adults and is consistent with the parent institution's mission and policies.
3. Demonstrate a knowledge and appreciation of literature for and by young adults in traditional and emerging formats.
4. Develop a collection of materials from a broad range of selection sources, and for a variety of reading skill levels, which encompasses all appropriate formats, including, but not limited to, media that reflect varied and emerging technologies, and materials in languages other than English.
5. Serve as a knowledgeable resource to schools in the community as well as parents and caregivers on materials for young adults.

Area VI. Access to Information.

The librarian will be able to:
1. Organize physical and virtual collections to maximize easy, equitable, and independent access to information by young adults.
2. Utilize current merchandising and promotional techniques to attract and invite young adults to use the collection.

3. Provide access to specialized information (i.e., community resources, work by local youth, etc.).

4. Formally and informally instruct young adults in basic research skills, including how to find, evaluate, and use information effectively.

5. Be an active partner in the development and implementation of technology and electronic resources to ensure young adults' access to knowledge and information.

6. Maintain awareness of ongoing technological advances and how they can improve access to information for young adults.

Area VII. Services.

The librarian will be able to:

1. Design, implement and evaluate programs and services within the framework of the library's strategic plan and based on the developmental needs of young adults and the public assets libraries represent, with young adult involvement whenever possible.

2. Identify and plan services with young adults in non-traditional settings, such as hospitals, home-school settings, alternative education, foster care programs, and detention facilities.

3. Provide a variety of informational and recreational services to meet the diverse needs and interests of young adults and to direct their own personal growth and development.

4. Continually identify trends and pop-culture interests of young people to inform and direct their recreational collection and programming needs.

5. Instruct young adults in basic information gathering, research skills, and information literacy skills—including those necessary to evaluate and use electronic information sources—to develop life-long learning habits.

6. Actively involve young adults in planning and implementing services and programs for their age group through advisory boards, task forces, and by less formal means (e.g., surveys, one-on-one discussion, focus groups, etc.).

7. Create an environment that embraces the flexible and changing nature of young adults' entertainment, technological, and informational needs.

Guide to Planning and Implementing a YALSA Program Session

January 2011

Introduction

Congratulations on being selected to present a program at ALA's Annual Conference! This planning guide is intended to help walk you through the process of planning a 90-minute program. In this guide you will find a step-by-step plan to building a successful program.

YALSA Program Goals and Objectives

Through its programs YALSA aims to:

- Further the continuing education of YALSA members
- Provide a forum through which YALSA members can actively learn about and participate in discussions on topics relevant to the profession
- Encourage the exchange of information and ideas and relationship building through networking
- Educate members on changes and developments in young adult librarianship

Adapted from: http://www.interpnet.com/download/NIWmanual.pdf

Designing an Effective Program

When planning your program, first determine who the audience is for your program. Secondly, decide what are your learning objectives. Thirdly, decide what you want your audience members to gain from the program. Whether presenting the program by yourself or with others, determine what concrete skills, programs, methods, or techniques you want that audience to take away from the program.

After you've completed these first three steps, begin to design an interactive session that supports these goals and objectives. Work to include real-world situations and examples in your session so that participants learn practical ideas and methods, which they can implement in their library.

When designing your program, make sure that you read the descriptor paragraph for your session and deliver on what is promised in the program descriptor. Participants choose which programs to attend based in large part on what is described in the program book, so make sure that your presentation aligns with the program descriptor.

For more information about suggested workshop activities, read "Presenter Tips" in Appendix B and please feel free to contact YALSA's Program Officer for Conferences and Events, Nichole Gilbert at ngilbert@ala.org or 1.800.545.2433 x4387.

Adult Learner Resources

The websites listed below can assist your taskforce in its early planning stages with designing an interactive session that meets the needs of adult learners.

http://codac.uoregon.edu/files/2011/01/Generations-in-the-Classroom-Handout.pdf

http://mti.missouri.edu/adult-education-literacy.php

http://wallacecenter.rit.edu/tls/teaching-learning-styles

ALA also provides some resources tailored to the library community through its LEARN Round Table: www.ala.org/ala/mgrps/rts/clenert/index.cfm

Presenting Your Program

Practice, practice, practice. Although this is simple advice, practicing your presentation is a critical component for a success program. Standing in front of an audience and presenting can be rather daunting even for the most adventurous of us. Knowing your presentation backwards and forwards and being comfortable with your supplemental material (PowerPoint, etc.) will help you feel confident and present a strong program.

If you are planning on using a PowerPoint, please do not read directly from the slides. Librarians do love to read, but reading from your Power-Point slides quickly puts your audience into a passive learning mode rather than being actively engaged in your presentation. Instead, use your Pow-erPoint to supplement your presentation. Keep your slides light on text and heavy on graphics. Choose high-quality graphics and a few key words that capture the idea or concept you are conveying. There are multiple websites where you can find free, high-quality graphics including, www.creativecommons.org.

Here are 10 quick tips to creating an effective PowerPoint presenta-tion: http://www.garrreynolds.com/Presentation/slides.html

During a Question and Answer session, please repeat the question asked before you answer it. Program rooms can be large and so it can be difficult for audience members to hear one another.

Please be aware that at ALA Annual, programs are run concurrently. Conference attendees will often leave early or come late to program ses-sions because they are trying to see and hear as many presentations as pos-sible. This movement of people in and out of the room may be distracting for some presenters, so again, practice your presentation many times over so that you are comfortable with it and less likely to be distracted.

Program Title & Description

Chose a title that generates interest in the event, but which clearly ar-ticulates the purpose of the workshop. Avoid overly cute or obscure titles. The YALSA Office may revise your content to address marketing concerns and/or space limits in printed programs. Please note that program descrip-tions are limited to 75 words. Include learning outcomes in the description as well as any confirmed speakers. The description should be written so that it piques the readers' interest but also that it provides key information succinctly.

Inviting Authors

All author invitations must be issued through the YALSA office. If you are interested in inviting an author to come and speak at your program ses-sion, please contact YALSA's Program Officer for Conferences and Events, Nichole Gilbert at ngilbert@ala.org or 1-800-545-2433 ext. 4387. Please note that publishers cover the cost of an author's appearance at a confer-ence event. YALSA does not pay for authors' travel or compensate them for speaking at events.

Logistics

Presenters

A list of presenters is due to YALSA's Program Officer for Conferences and Events immediately following the Midwinter Meeting for the ALA Annual Conference program book. The presenter list should be updated on YALSA's wiki if any speakers are added at a later date.

Room Setup

Please do not change the arrangement of chairs or tables in the room. YALSA incurs a fee anytime a room setup is changed.

Materials for your meeting will arrive one hour prior to the start of your meeting. Since meeting rooms have multiple sessions scheduled throughout the day, materials cannot be delivered more than one hour in advance of your meeting.

YALSA recommends that handouts are placed at the back of the meeting room. This allows participants to gather handouts without disturbing other program attendees.

Handouts

Handouts are intended to enhance or to concisely summarize the presentation, but not to duplicate the presentation. They are still popular with participants because they are a simple tool they can use to show their boss or coworkers a part of what they learned at the event. Handouts that are popular with participants include annotated bibliographies and lists of resources where they can go to learn more on the topic. As a part of its effort to be environmentally responsible, YALSA will not print a PowerPoint presentation as a handout.

All handouts etc. are due to YALSA⊠s Program Officer for Conferences and Events no later than **six weeks** before the event.

ALA/YALSA has a space for sharing presentation related resources and materials at http://presentations.ala.org. Please upload your handouts to this site.

Audio/Visual

YALSA's Program Officer for Conferences and Events will oversee the ordering of all AV equipment for a YALSA workshop. Please contact Nichole Gilbert (ngilbert@ala.org) for your AV equipment needs.

AV requests are due by February 15. Please note: No late AV requests can be accommodated due to cost.

Please include any requests for audio or Internet access requests in your AV request form.

Please do not order any additional AV on-site; this is extremely costly to YALSA. Only YALSA's Program Officer for Conferences and Events has the authority to do this.

Please note that Internet access is dependent on the conference center/hotel that your meeting takes place in. YALSA cannot guarantee Internet access for your meeting.

If you require a laptop for your presentation, please arrange to bring your own. YALSA cannot provide laptops for presenters.

First Aid

There is a first aid station at the convention center. YALSA's Program Officer for Conferences and Events will provide contact and location information of the station to the preconference chair when it becomes available.

Internet Access

ALA, not YALSA, determines the location of the meeting room. If it is placed in the convention center, free wireless Internet access should be available in the room. If it is placed at another location, free wireless Internet access will probably not be available. For this reason, YALSA does not recommend live streaming of the Internet as a part of a program presentation. Please include requests for Internet access in your AV equipment request.

Canceling a Session

In the event that you are not able to present your session at conference, please contact YALSA's Program Officer for Conference and Events immediately to work on finding a replacement presenter for your session.

Publicity & Marketing

YALSA will publicize Annual conference programs via YALSA's web presence. Presenters are encouraged to market their conference program on the regional and local level.

Rights & Permissions

YALSA has the right to publish all publications, products, and/or presentations created by committees or connected to committee-sponsored activities and programs.

You are responsible for ensuring that the content of your presentation, handouts, etc. does not contain copyrighted material, and you are expected to appropriately cite sources wherever your content isn't original.

Travel, Housing, Registration

Please note that ALA/YALSA does not compensate or cover travel, housing, or conference registration costs for librarians/library workers for presenting at conference. There are many non-monetary benefits to presenting for YALSA. Please see "Benefits of Speaking at YALSA Programs" at the end of this guide, and be sure to share that with potential speakers.

YALSA Staff Contact Information

YALSA Office: 1-800-545-2433 ext. 4390 or yalsa@ala.org

Complete contact information for each staff member is at: www.ala.org/ala/mgrps/divs/yalsa/aboutyalsa/staff.cfm

Content adapted from ASAE and the Center Technology Conference and Expo 2010 Content Leader Manual. http://www.asaecenter.org/files/Tech2010ContentLeaderManual.pdf

Appendix A - Benefits of Speaking at YALSA Programs

New opportunities: Speakers often find that participation in a YALSA program leads to requests to speak at other conferences, events, or workshops; invitations to publish; or opportunities to do consulting work.

Information sharing: You will have the unique opportunity to showcase your research and/or best practices to a captive audience of young adult librarians, library media specialists, graduate students, researchers, and educators from around the country.

Speakers can display any promotional materials on a table in the back of the event room and/or can upload materials on YALSA's wiki at http://wikis.ala.org/yalsa and on ALA's wiki at http://presentations.ala.org.

Networking: You will be able to network with hundreds of the most influential individuals in the field of young adult librarianship as well as thousands of library and information professionals from around the world.

Attendance at ALA's Annual Conference ranges from about 20,000 to 28,000.

Prestige: The prestige of being selected to present at a YALSA event.

You have an opportunity to set yourself apart and enhance your credibility and stature among professionals.

Personal growth: Refresh and increase your personal knowledge. Challenge yourself (and your colleagues) through lively debates and interactive sessions.

Contribute to the greater good of the profession: Raise awareness about your passion. Plant the seed for change and growth.

Appendix B - YALSA Presenter Tips (or how not to be a talking head)

Understanding Adult Learners

- Adult learners crave learning environments that engage the senses and stimulate the intellect.
- They see learning as a means to an end, not an end in and of itself.
- They seek to learn something they need to accomplish a goal or do their work.

Adult Learners Need

- to know WHY to do it (meaning how they will benefit from changing the way they currently do things)
- to know HOW to do it
- to PRACTICE doing it
- to SHARE what they know with other learners in the room

We Learn and Retain

- 10% of what we READ
- 20% of what we HEAR
- 30% of what we SEE
- 50% of what we SEE and HEAR
- 70% of what is DISCUSSED

The basics of your presentation

Create a solid opener (story, comedy, hard-hitting fact).

Develop content that is geared toward the audience. Keep the material short, applicable, interesting, and pertinent.

Plan for fun energizers several times throughout (depending on length of presentation).

Put together brief but useful handouts.

Come up with a closer that brings it all home and provides for take-away value.

If there will be co-presenters

Many presentations are successful because they incorporate several perspectives, i.e., several speakers or a panel.

The downside to this is the panel members may not know one another.

Share materials well in advance so you have appropriate segues, etc.

Talk (if possible, meet) as many times as needed to get it flawless ahead of time!

Know Your Audience

How many people will be in the audience? 20? 100? 200?

Adjust along the way, if necessary. Ask for a show of hands at the opening to ascertain expertise level and comfort level with your topic.

Establish rapport. The audience is why you're there. Let them know they're important.

Gauge the general mood that day and make adjustments if necessary.

Deliver on Your Promise

Read the description of how your presentation was marketed and refer back to this as you prepare your presentation.

Tell your audience what you are going to talk about and provide a few goals and objectives for the session.

Tell them what you have just told them. Repeat your most important points three times in three different ways.

Incorporate Interaction

"Be a guide on the side, not a sage on the stage." Strive to incorporate one interactive component for at least every two hours of lecture. Some examples:

- Case studies
- Simulations
- Small group discussions

Use questioning techniques to stimulate thinking, challenge beliefs, probe opinions, clarify implications, and promote conclusions.

Be sure to allow "wait time" after asking a question. Pause and allow for people to digest the question and choose to respond. Several seconds of silence is okay.

Even a show of hands is a type of interaction.

Vary the Format

Accommodate different learning styles helps keep the audience interested.

Visual: video clips, graphs, charts, photos

Audio: music, brief audio interview, sound effects

Group activities: role play, discussion, hands-on, physical activity.

- Ask learners to provide their own examples.
- Relate training to something they know.
- Ask for feedback throughout the session.
- Get their ideas and ask for their input.

Start with an Opener

This breaks the preoccupation of the audience, gets their attention, and sets the tone of the program

Types of openers:

- Discuss an incident that relates to the topic.
- Ask a broad question.
- Ask for a quick show of hands.
- Share something that makes them laugh.
- Make an outrageous (but not inappropriate) statement.

Energize the Audience

Even in a short presentation, energy can drain from the room. If you feel the energy wane, think about an energizer. It gets the audience moving, talking to new people, etc. and helps audience members bond with one another.

Types of energizers:

- Ask a question. Have people stand up if they are answering "Yes."
- Ask participants to have a brief talk with someone else at their table or row on a topic you assign them (discussion could be as brief as one minute).
- Pre-content quiz (can also help you gauge the audience).
- Quick video segment
- Ask for a volunteer
- Ice breaker (ask an interesting or unusual question for pairs to answer)

Bring Closure to the Presentation

This gives the audience a chance to connect the dots and allows for action planning.

Types of closers:

- Story. Can go back to the opening story and "close" it out.
- Action planning. Give a charge or mission to the group.

- Provide take-home value. Literally ask the audience, "What are three things you learned today that you can implement tomorrow?"
- Have an actual quiz to review the material (consider giving out prizes).

Provide Great Handouts

Keep the formatting simple and uncluttered

Types of handouts:

- Case studies
- Charts, diagrams and graphs
- Checklists
- Annotated bibliographies

Tips for Dealing with Tough Audiences

Turn difficult situations and comments back to the group. Allow group members to work through the situations themselves.

- Avoid expressing personal opinions.
- NEVER argue with a participant.

If necessary, remind people to turn off their electronic devices, or ask them to leave the room if they must use them.

Appeal to their enlightened self-interest, or what's in it for them: how this will make their work easier, advance their career, and/or make their work more rewarding.

Appeal to their idealism: explain the importance of the training in the context of their customers (e.g., young adults) and to their institution.

Remember that it's okay to have fun! Be sure to use some or all of these in your presentation:

- Humor
- Games
- Prizes
- Icebreakers
- Music

—Content adapted from a PowerPoint presentation by ASAE staff for the 2009 Great Ideas Conference

A *Library Journal* Mover & Shaker, Monique Delatte Starkey is an associate professor at Fullerton College and an adjunct for Rio Hondo College. Delatte Starkey worked in teen services for over five years with the County of Los Angeles Public Library. She has authored and co-authored over $100,000 in grants for libraries. Sponsored by Fullerton College and YALSA as a member of the 2011 cohort of ALA Emerging Leaders, Monique began taking advantage of the opportunities available with YALSA through publication in *Excellence in Library Services to Young Adults*. Monique continued to publish with YALSA via *Young Adult Library Services Journal* and *Cool Teen Programs Under $100*. Delatte Starkey also teaches four-week online YALSA courses including *Growing, Managing, and Defending the Young Adult Budget*.

Vegetarian strawbrarian Delatte Starkey lives in Belmont Heights, SoCal, with her husband David, five frisky foster felines, and their neighbors' three cats: White Cat, Grey Cat, and Orange Twitchy Cat.

Reach the author via MoniqueDelatteStarkey.com.